COUNTER-STATEMENT

/

COUNTER-STATEMENT

BY

KENNETH BURKE

UNIVERSITY OF CALIFORNIA PRESS

Berkeley, Los Angeles, London

UNIVERSITY OF CALIFORNIA PRESS
Berkeley and Los Angeles, California

UNIVERSITY OF CALIFORNIA PRESS, LTD.
London, England

Library of Congress Catalog Card Number: 68-20356
First California printing, 1968
ISBN 0-520-00196-6

(A cloth-bound edition of this work is available
from Hermes Publications, Los Altos, California.)

Printed in the United States of America

3 4 5 6 7 8 9

PREFACE TO THE FIRST EDITION

Perhaps it should be said, by way of preface, that this book does not set itself up as an "attack." It deals but secondarily and sporadically with refutation. We have chosen to call it *Counter-Statement* solely because—as regards its basic concerns and tenets—each principle it advocates is matched by an opposite principle flourishing and triumphant today. Heresies and orthodoxies will always be changing places, but whatever the minority view happens to be at any given time, one must consider it as "counter." Hence the title—which will not, we hope, suggest either an eagerness for the fray or a sense of defeat.

There is pamphleteering; there is inquiry. In so far as an age is bent, a writer establishes equilibrium by leaning (leaning either as his age leans, or in the direction opposite to his age)—and this we might call "pamphleteering." A writer will also desire to develop an equilibrium of his own, regardless of external resistances—and this we might call "inquiry." His actual work will probably show an indeterminate wavering between the two positions; he himself will not be sure just when he is inquiring and when pamphleteering. And he may not be wholly satisfied by the thought of doing exclusively either.

We recall a book on diet which, though it gave stern precepts against over-eating, went on to suggest that one should glut himself on occasion lest he become so inept at managing large quantities of food that he risk insulting his host at a banquet. And perhaps by a similar discrepancy, though cherishing the ideal of inquiry (or sober eating), we should occasionally dip into pamphleteering (or gluttony) in order that so biologic a weapon (for snatching a livelihood from the jungles of society) be not wholly lost through disuse. Once one has pamphleteered, however, dare he not in revision try, even at the risk of canceling himself, to transform the contentious into the speculative? In any event, one must admit that in matters of strength and affirmativeness even the most impulsive literature is a very poor second to brickbats—so it might be better to leave strength and affirmativeness for waylaying a man, and to seek other qualities when writing.

These essays, read in their present order, should serve to elucidate a point of view. This point of view is somewhat apologetic, negativistic, and even antinomian, as regards everything but art. It is not antinomian as regards art because of a feeling that art is naturally antinomian. Art's very accumulation (its discordant voices arising out of many systems) serves to undermine any one rigid scheme of living— and herein lies "wickedness" enough.

Of the writers we discuss, particularly of those we discuss at length (De Gourmont, Pater, Flaubert, Thomas Mann, André Gide) we attempt to emphasize such methods and inclinations as bear upon the issues treated in the more theoretic chapters. Perhaps, in showing what these writers *stand for*, we do not always show what they *are*. But when dealing with men whose work is so generally known, one may legitimately be interpretive rather than informative.

The two chapters, "Psychology and Form" and "The Poetic Process," handle somewhat songfully issues which we later discuss in a more clinical fashion.

"The Status of Art" is an attempt to consider various doctrines which have—since the time of Kant—served to bolster up the "detractors" of art. Several doctrines have come into prominence which seemed to make art questionable—and the essay aims in turn to make these doctrines questionable. It does not propose to set up a rival list of "glorifications."

The "Program" proposes to trace the possible political and economic implications of an attitude which—so far as our primary concerns go—is not political or economic at all. But any scheme of thinking or living must obviously require some specific social structure—and the "Program" seeks to consider, in a general way, what this social structure would have to become if our principles were to prevail: what, in other words, could be the particular practical results of this particular "æsthetic."

As for our set-piece, the "Lexicon Rhetoricæ," it is frankly intended as a machine—machine for criticism, however, not for poetry (which, as someone has said, is always beyond the last formula). It is a kind of judgment machine, designed to serve as an instrument for clarifying critical issues (not so much for settling issues as for making the nature of a controversy more definite). It seeks to perform this function by working out a set of "pivotal" or "key" terms for discussing the processes of literary appeal. It should be a critical nomenclature for paralleling in analytic terms what a work of art itself performs in terms of the "creative," the "imaginative." It is, in general, an attempt to schematize many critical concepts which have been more or less vaguely in the air since psychology took the place of metaphysics as a foundation for æsthetic theory. It also contains a more or less covert attack upon certain critical assumptions of the day, fostered by those who mistake biography for life and usually insist that one write a book as though he were ordering groceries. For the conveying of information about politics, burglaries, trade markets, new comets, and outraged husbands, our newspapers have a very satisfactorily developed technique—and by far the major portion of the world's communications can be adequately couched in this medium. But of the remainder,

COUNTER-STATEMENT

some fraction may deserve more formal treatment — and gently, deviously, our "Lexicon" pleads for the restoration of stylistic procedures which will avoid not only the vices, but also the virtues, of journalism. And our "Lexicon" would not for the world make literature and life synonymous since, by comparison in such terms, the meanest life is so overwhelmingly superior to the noblest poem that illiteracy becomes almost a moral obligation. Rather, our "Lexicon" would look upon literature as the thing added—the little white houses in a valley that was once a wilderness.

KENNETH BURKE

ANDOVER, NEW JERSEY
June, 1931

See later preface, xv, for comment on this.

PREFACE TO THE SECOND EDITION

Looking back over this book, which was originally published twenty years ago, and some parts of which were written more than thirty years ago, I have the "mixed feelings" that usually mark such an experience. There are some youthful, jaunty, even cocksure moments here. But one consideration fills me with unqualified delight. I refer to the fact that the book begins on the word "perhaps" and ends on the word "norm." True, the perhaps-sayer can become in his way as emphatic as yea-sayers and nay-sayers do in theirs (when he dodges among yeas and nays of his own). And the quest of the norm must bring one to feel great sympathy, and even kinship, with many kinds of "abnorm." But the over-all trend is *through* Perhaps *towards* the norm (even though I unconsciously revealed my tentativeness with regard to it by ending on it—not outright, but in quotation marks).

Add the theory of form that is developed in these pages (it is summarized in a few lines on page 124)—and I believe you have, in these three moments, the gist of this book, and maybe also of the books by me that grew out of it.

The Perhaps, in time, led to the notion that society's nouns need many adjectives, and its verbs many adverbs. Or, otherwise put, the attempt was made later to turn from "inconsistency" to a systematic search for a dialectic of many voices. The quest of the "norm" led to a study of the varied ways in which men seek by symbolic means to make themselves at home in social tensions. And the theory of form led to problems that, while they may seem to some readers far from this theory, are logical developments from it.

As regards art in particular, and speculative expression in

general, there are these two possible opposing views, when we are considering the relationship between art and society:

There is the "censorship" principle, and there is the "lightning rod" principle. Those who think by the "censorship" principle can find their best source in Plato's *Republic*, whereas I would interpret Aristotle's Poetics as basically "lightning rod." Censorship implies a one-to-one relation between expression and society. In this view (to borrow an example from Plato) if you wanted to "coordinate" a society by building up a warlike group, you might decide that its members should hear only warlike music. The kind of expression you chose would thus pump them full of warlike imagery, on the assumption that, as thus directly conditioned, they would respond by spontaneously favoring warlike attitudes.

In contrast with this strongly "totalitarian" view of art and thinking, there is a more complex "liberal" view. "Purification," in this scheme, is got by the draining-off of dangerous charges, as lightning rods are designed, not to "suppress" danger, but to draw it into harmless channels.

I take this to be the principle implicit in Aristotle's view of tragedy, his somewhat homœopathic notion that we are cleansed of emotional tensions by kinds of art deliberately designed to affect us with these tensions under controlled conditions.

For short periods, unquestionably, the principle of conditioning, or coordination by censorship, is very effective, particularly now, when people generally have not yet learned how to discount the motivational powers of the new mass media. But it is my contention that a society is protected in the long run only by the more liberal principle. And I had such a condition in mind when I referred, at one point, to "the cultural value of fear, distrust, and hypochondria." I had in mind here the kind of uncertainty, or even uneasiness, that goes with a Cult of the Perhaps, and with its corresponding Method. I most decidedly did not mean that there is any hope in mass hysterias engineered by demagogues who are in turn assisted by efficient control over the channels of information and communication.

The sort of fear I had in mind, for example, concerned the attitude towards the "promises" of applied science. More and more people, in recent years, are coming to realize that technology can be as ominous as it is promising. Such fear, if properly rationalized, is but the kind of discretion a society should have with regard to all new powers.

One chapter in this book I inserted with the deliberate intention that it should soon be outmoded. Or rather, I did not expect it to win *literal* adherents, even at the time when it was published. I refer to my "Program," a hypothetical translation of Bohemianism, or Æstheticism, into its corresponding political equivalents, as though one were proposing planks for the platform of a national "Art Party." Yet I believe you might find it serviceable, if you will take it not literally, but as an impressionistic portrait of the motivational tangle that besets our nation, plaguing political leaders who would unite nationwide parties; and I submit that this tangle of motives also affects the temper of even our artistic spokesmen who are not specifically concerned with such problems.

Ideally, I suppose, the chapter should have been written not as by one speaker, but as a dialogue in which several speakers conflictingly participated. The representative of "the æsthetic" could have been a lean and scurvy fellow who blurted out things in a somewhat violent fashion. "The practical" could have been represented by a portly, not wholly articulate gentleman, of obviously high repute, who looked upon his adversary as a scandal. And there should have been at least one other figure, somewhat drooping, who suffered the wrangling of the two, while feeling that both had their particular kinds of justification.

COUNTER-STATEMENT

The chapter on "The Status of Art," at some points, wins victories a bit too easily. As for my remarks on Spengler, I should add: Spengler made a tremendous impression upon me. He scared me, much as the Theatre Guild's production of Capek's *R.U.R.* scared me, or much as a child (or the child in our adult selves) is scared by the story of some monstrous invader from an alien planet. No, he scared me even more than that; for he pictured an invader already here, from within (an invader derived from mankind's best logic, mankind's best genius). When "disposing" of Spengler with such dispatch, I could have been more judicious by paying tribute to his powers as a rhetorician. Eventually, I worked out a compromise of this sort: I decided that the high development of modern technology might change the rules somewhat; accordingly, conditions that are "normal" to our society would probably have been *fatal* to societies in which there was a much smaller percentage of technology.

When speaking of "the Rooseveltian mind" (p. 102), I referred to T. R., the lion-hunter.

There are many passages in this book (particularly in the earliest chapters) which I would now phrase quite differently. That is, though I might want to retain the *idea*, I would modify the *attitude* that went along with it.

Perhaps the most complicated kind of revision is required in my reference to De Gourmont as a writer who "recognized" that the basis of the First World War, "as of every war," was "the pugnacity natural to all individual or collective egos." The passage continued: "He blamed the war on militarism, although militarism to De Gourmont was not a term in economics; De Gourmont could always talk more enthusiastically of man in comparison with his analysis of a sea mollusc than he could from consideration of the industrial revolution. Essentially, the war for him, aside from the painful fact that it was his own personal friends who were dying, was not different from an unwritten event of pre-history, a struggle with clubs."

Any reduction of *social* motives to terms of sheer "nature" would now seem to me a major error. Naturalism has served as deceptively in the modern world as supernaturalism ever did in the past, to misrepresent motives that are intrinsic to the social order. In recent decades, this deception has been all the greater, since it borrows persuasiveness from the prestige of the natural sciences and their pragmatic sanction.

For the whole story, we would add this extra coordinate, for which we have chosen the unwieldy name of the "socioanagogic." The word is intended to sum up the ways in which things of the senses are secretly emblematic of motives in the social order, so that all visible, tangible entities become an enigma, and materials become a pageantry, or what Diderot, in his *Neveu de Rameau*, called "pantomime."

Also, in keeping with my later cryptological interests, on looking over the original Preface I'd incline to ponder now the closing reference to literature as "the thing added—the little white houses in a valley that was once a wilderness." I'd incline to ask: "How does this writer use 'white', 'houses', 'valley', and 'wilderness', in other contexts?" And I'd wonder whether he had had remotely in mind the line in the Sonnets: "By adding one thing to my purpose nothing."

*   *   *

Once, at a party, when I was talking with a friend, another guest came up and said to me, brightly: "I saw an early book of yours in a second-hand store, and I bought it." Then he added, "It's a first edition. The first edition of that book is rare, isn't it?" Whereat my friend piped up: "The second edition is still rarer." (I always believed in having friends who help one keep in trim.)

COUNTER-STATEMENT

Anyhow, here is a second edition of *Counter-Statement*.
Would that I could say: "How different are the times
now!" For this book was published, and a large portion of
it was written, during a period of stress that forced upon all
of us the need to decide exactly wherein the worth and
efficacy of a literary work reside. And here we are, confronting another set of such tensions now.

K.B.

ANDOVER, NEW JERSEY
September, 1952

Mass media new
(see pg xii).

CONTENTS

THREE ADEPTS OF "PURE" LITERATURE

WHEN, after about fifty years of letter writing, Flaubert saw for the first time the correspondence of Balzac, he was reasonably disgusted. Here was a man who had followed — to Flaubert's way of thinking, at least — the most glorious trade in the world, and yet whose private communications showed not the least concern with art. The love of the general which distinguished Flaubert was completely lacking; in its place there was a preponderance of minutely personal debits and credits. The novel, to Balzac, performed the same functions as politics or the stock market: it was intended to procure for him some considerable social station, to make him a Parisian celebrity.

Flaubert had always looked upon art as an existence-in-itself. *"L'art est assez vaste pour occuper tout un homme,"* he had written to one friend who was evidently getting a good deal of complacency out of fast living. Shakespeare he found "not a man, but a continent." He seemed to feel that the artist closed one door and opened another, that the artist possessed something unintelligible to the non-artist. Flaubert, in his own bulky, broad-shouldered way, was of the *tour d'ivoire* school of writers. Art was something to live in, like Shakespeare, like a continent. In his first letter, written at the age of nine, he tells of writing comedies. In the next it is novels, while the third mentions *"des histoirre"* (sic!). The first also speaks of New Year's Day as *"bête,"* thus giving the substance of about sixty years' correspondence. Flaubert was born in 1821; by 1835 he had a pseudonym: Gustave Antuoskothi Koclott.

We enter a highly documented adolescence. If, as it is said

often enough, everyone has the making of an artist as a child, it is even truer that everyone has the artist's temper as an adolescent. In revenge, when studying the adolescence of an artist like Flaubert, who was not only not precocious, but had shown signs almost of imbecility during childhood, one finds himself in a well-tracked labyrinth. One might catalogue the phase, briefly, thus:

a) *The cult of the illicit.* ("Also, I admire Nero; he is the culminating figure of the antique world. Woe to that man who does not quake in reading Suetonius! Recently I read the life of Heliogabalus in Plutarch. He has a different beauty from that of Nero. He is more Asiatic, more feverish, more romantic, more unbridled. He is the evening of the day; he is a delirium of torches; but Nero is more calm, more beautiful, more antique, more poised, all told, superior.")

b) *The cynicism of analysis.* ("I dissect unceasingly; that gives me amusement; and when finally I have uncovered the corruption in something which was thought pure, the gangrene of lovely places, I raise my head and laugh.")

c) *Diffusion, frustration, renunciation.* ("Oh, how much I would give to be either more stupid or more clever, atheist or mystic, but something complete and entire, an identity, *something,* in short." Or, "I dreamed of glory when I was a mere child, and now I do not even have the pride of mediocrity . . . as to writing, I have renounced it totally.")

d) *Exuberance of conceptions, intoxication of talk, love of plenitude.* ("I want a mass of fun, of riot, of violent activity, the whole thing dumped *pêle-mêle,* in a heap, without order, without style, as when we talk together, and the conversation walks, runs, gambols, when we become elated, when we burst out laughing, et cetera.")

e) *Escape.* ("Oh! if I had a tent made of reeds and bamboo, along the shore of the Ganges, how I would listen all night to the noise of the water in the rushes, to the cooing

2

of birds perched on the yellow trees." A nostalgia for which poor Emma Bovary was to suffer some years later.)

f) Insanity. ("A few days ago I met three poor idiots who were begging; they were hideous, revolting with ugliness and cretinism; they could not talk; they could scarcely walk. On seeing me they began making signs that they loved me; they smiled, put their hands to their faces, and threw me kisses. At Pont-l'Evêque my father owns a farm, the caretaker of which has an imbecile daughter. The first time she saw me she also evinced a strange attachment. I attract animals and the insane." Also, calling to wit his earlier *Mémoires d'un Fou.*)

This may not be the adolescence of everyone. But it is certainly the adolescence both of those who knock and are admitted and of those who knock and are not admitted. Some, becoming sensible with years, outgrow it. More or less sullenly, the artist retains it. In any case, Flaubert went no further; his work is a refinement, a subtilization, of this equipment.

The elations and renunciations, with time, were patiently beaten down to a minimum; in 1845 he wrote, although perhaps a little hastily, "I notice that I rarely laugh now and that I am no longer unhappy; I have matured." This was part of Flaubert's Potsdamnation of the spirit. After *La Tentation de Saint-Antoine,* we see his method becoming steadily more deliberate, until, in writing *Bouvard et Pécuchet,* he read one thousand five hundred books to produce one. "One must write more *coldly,*" he advised Louise Colet, his much-neglected mistress, and an admirer of Flaubert's arch-anathema, De Musset; "Let us distrust that sort of warmth which is called inspiration and in which nervous emotion figures much more prominently than muscle." This distrust of the "poetic" method of attack, however, did not modify the background of his interests, which retained their adolescent warmth. Along with his insistence that art be given "with methodical relentlessness, the *precision* of the physical sciences," one finds an almost naïve joy in expurganda. He writes, for instance, to the De Goncourts while working on *Salammbô*, "*Ainsi je suis parvenu dans le même chapitre à amener successivement une pluie de m——*(sic) *et une procession de pédérastes*."

There is also the possibility, however, that the pugnacity of Flaubert's material came of an instinctive demand that he arrest his readers in spite of himself. In any case, it is true that he reached his public in just this way. *Madame Bovary* could hardly have set a nation to buzzing over its technical triumphs of form and its microscopic style: this was accomplished by the prosecution for obscenity. *Salammbô,* in like manner, created its stir among outraged archæologists and moralists protesting against the paganism involved. *La Tentation de Saint-Antoine* was the occasion of sermons preached against the author, and *L'Education Sentimentale* was so redoubted for its treatment of political issues that of the hundred and fifty persons to whom he sent complimentary copies only thirty dared answer him! ... Thus, we have the phenomenon of a man who was deeply interested in things imperceptible—and completely immaterial—to practically his entire public, and yet who, for purely extrinsic reasons, acquired an almost academic pre-eminence.

Between adolescence and the formal sitting down to a life of writing, Flaubert passed through one more tentative period, his first trip to the Near East. Error, unwieldy ruins, the human herd trampling the human herd, prostitution, corruption; we see his preference for contemplating things of this nature, a preference which was to justify itself later in *Salammbô,* while his most penetrating letters are written from the Nile, where history had been envisaged minutely and commemorated by the colossal, a distinctly Flaubertian process. On returning to France, he wrote his first *Tentation de Saint-Antoine,* and then began *Madame Bovary.* From now on he settled definitely into a monotonous life, fulfilling his own requirement that the artist "live as a bourgeois and think as a demi-god," and putting art as the matter of prime importance in life. He would delay seeing Louise Colet for even months, until he had "finished a chapter," and when she became too importunate he dismissed her entirely. Until about 1870, whatever minor incidents occurred did not produce any noticeable change in his attitudes. From the time of the Franco-Prussian War, however, he became decidedly more acrid, at times even querulous. One by one his friends died off, leaving him lonely, and with a sense of superannuation, of sacrificing himself to an ideal now universally betrayed. His own constitution was ruined; he suffered from headaches and nausea. In 1880 he died suddenly of apoplexy, while engaged in the most enormous of all his enormous labours, *Bouvard et Pécuchet.*

I have not, up to this point, discussed the really essential subject of the letters: the relation they bear to the study of his æsthetic. The final testimony of the letters seems to be that Flaubert never succeeded in arriving at an æsthetic amenable to his temperament. Indeed, the very fact that he did not write the low-visioned letters of Balzac is a testimony. Balzac had reached a complete expression in his art; therefore he felt no need of putting anything other than his personal ambitions and disappointments into his correspondence. Flaubert, on the contrary, sensed an unconscious need of some complement to his fiction. I do not mean to signify by this that Flaubert's work is inferior to that of Balzac. Balzac had the brain of a petty official, and wrote like one. Flaubert had something about him of that quality he attributed to the greatest masterpieces, a sort of slow "stupidity," like the products of nature, like animals and mountains. He was, as he said of himself magnificently, *"bas, bouffon, obscène tant que tu voudras, mais lugubre nonobstant."*

The most striking implication of the letters with respect to his literary methods is that his medium was not adapted to the effects he most desired. "I incline a good deal towards criticism. The novel I have been writing has been sharpening that faculty of mine, because it is above all else a work of criticism, or even of anatomy." And he adds this tremendous heresy against his own work-shop: "The reader will not be aware, I hope, of all the psychological travail hidden beneath the form, but he will sense the effect." Is it any wonder that he said of the book after it was published, *"Tout ce que j'aime n'y est pas."* Yet why should everything he loves in a book be lacking? Or why should he want to conceal the "psychological travail," which was a distinctive aspect of the book? *"On me croit épris du réel, tandis que je l'exècre; car c'est en haine du réalisme que j'ai entrepris ce roman."* The book (*Madame Bovary*) was written, he goes on to say, *par parti pris;* the rest was incidental.

A letter, written in 1852, brings out his difficulties most plainly:

"What seems beautiful to me, what I should most like to do, would be a book about nothing, a book without any exterior tie, but sustained by the internal force of its style ... a book which would have almost no subject, or at least in which the subject would be almost invisible, if that is possible. The most beautiful works are those with the least matter. ... I believe the future of art is in these channels."

And twenty-four years later, in a letter to George Sand, we find him saying:

"I remember what poundings of the heart I experienced, what keen pleasure I felt, on beholding a bare wall of the Acropolis. ... *Eh bien!* I wonder if a book, independently of what it says, might produce the same effect? In the precision of its groupings, the rarity of its materials, the unction, the general harmony—is there not some intrinsic virtue here, . . . something eternal as a principle?"

No wonder Flaubert finished each successive book with a feeling of frustration, of revulsion. No wonder he complained that he wrote like someone playing the piano with a ball of lead on every knuckle. He might, in speculation, consider an art of methodological triumph, an art free of all subject-matter—but meanwhile he devoted years on end to the patient accumulation of detail, of those minute accuracies which his disciples look upon as the basis of his intentions (and which he himself, even at a moment of faith in them, called of secondary importance). The anomaly of the situation would have wearied any but this ox of art.

He finds himself midway between two contradictory attitudes: one, a love of "mouthings, lyricism, the flying of big birds, the *sonorities* of prose"; the other, a desire to make the reader feel his books "almost materially." Despite his many art-to-display-art preferences, he was attempting to write under an art-to-conceal-art æsthetic. A writer who (as he said of himself with a frankness which men less sure of themselves would avoid) "loved the glitter as much as the gold," he was using the *genre* in which glitter is most an obstacle, the *genre* wherein one can be rhetorically brilliant only by subterfuge, or by endangering the purity of one's effect. The novel makes of literature the verbalization of *experience,* the conversion of *life* into diction—whereas Flaubert, with his pronounced interest in the absolute effects of art, would make of literature the *verbalization* of experience, the conversion of life into *diction*. An admirer of Shakespeare, of Château-briand, he was attempting to write in the æsthetic of a Stendhal.

Now, Stendhal as a novelist despised the protrusion of art;

his greatest ambition was to write sentences which could make the reader forget them as sentences. He perfected the novel of vicarious existence, the novel which one reads not as literature, but as a substitute for living. Stendhal, if he were writing Hugo's *L'Homme Qui Rit,* would begin by eliminating every saliency of conceit, paradox, antinome, metaphor, which makes this work astonishing. He would destroy it as the obviously "literary" masterpiece it now is, would shun all effects likely to remind the reader that the book is "written." Whatever the virtues of such a method, it is ill adjusted to a man who loves sentences as sentences, not as mere instruments to an end but as ends in themselves.

Flaubert's nearest approach to the less realistic and more declamatory aspects of fiction was his *Tentation de Saint-Antoine.* Its gorgeous dreams are theatrical, even spectacular —and the references to this work in the *Correspondence* are significant. The nausea associated with the writing of his other works indicates something more fundamental than the mere annoyance of constructing a book. It indicates an error in first principles, in the underlying procedure whereby, even though the work is a masterpiece of its kind (as *Madame Bovary*) its attainments cannot give the artist satisfactions commensurate with the efforts involved. But in the case of the Temptation the evidence is different. Instead of nausea, conflict, herculean conquest, we find him saying: "will the good days of Saint Anthony return?" In this work, he remarks elsewhere, he was at home, he "had only to proceed." "But I may never know again," he adds, "such *éperduments de style* as I got for myself during those eighteen magnificent months. With what zest I collected the pearls of this necklace!"

The nature of Flaubert's problems was obscured, I think, by the Platonic vocabulary in which he couched them. A distinction between "pure form" and "pure matter" may enable

8

one to speculate about books which talk beautifully about nothing, but it provides no hints at all for specific matters of methodology. Distinctions between art to conceal art and art to display art, between the realistic and the declamatory, observation and ritual, information and ceremony, might be more discussable. They will also, I fear, serve to make most readers feel that Flaubert was "right" in suppressing the verbalistic side of his interests. For though we read in our journals thousands of informative words each day, though it is the highest ambition of these words to be "imperceptible," and though they become "perceptible" only when the haste of their author leads to faulty construction, most of us require the same "clarity" in even our most artistic prose. As for Flaubert, his choice seems to have led him finally into a kind of prose the virtues of which lay primarily in avoidances (avoidances of too many *of*'s, avoidances of ambiguity to do with the antecedents of pronouns, avoidances of phrasing unsuited to his respiration, avoidances of vowel combinations awkward to the tongue). His choice precluded his development into the aggressively "written" style of a Hugo, for whom he nonetheless had an almost abject awe. And the Correspondence would indicate that Flaubert was not happy with his choice.

II

Whatever our reservations as to Walter Pater, we must recognize his superior adjustment of technique to æsthetic interests. An unenterprising thinker, an inveterate borrower of other men's ideas, concerned with a probably non-existent past, he was more of an "innovator" than many of his outstanding contemporaries who gave great thought to innovation. Without the slightest element of "rebellion," he shaped prose fiction to his purposes. In this he was undoubtedly assisted by his wide reading in Greek and Roman literature, which was rarely "lifelike" as that word was understood by nineteenth-century novelists. He also had in his favor the limitations of his personality. Being an oddity but untroubled, being exceptional without strain, he could simplify his work through sheer lack of sympathy for anything but the restricted world in which he lived. Yet his cloistered existence at Oxford, while removing him from the specific issues of his times, permitted him to hear discussed the various key ideas underlying these issues; accordingly, though he derived the characters and environments of his fictions by research, the basic forms of experience which they exemplify treat of the same tendencies as the works of artists less retiring. And his spontaneous interests enabled him to parallel the interests of his times in another way: his love of twilight, of emergence and evanescence, equipped him to symbolize transition.

In the sixth chapter of *Gaston de Latour* we can trace Pater's method with unusual accuracy, partially no doubt because this chapter, never having received a final revision, readily betrays its articulations. He begins:

"We all feel, I suppose, the pathos of that mystic situation in Homer, where the Greeks at the last throb of battle around the body of Patroclus find the horror of supernatural darkness added to their other foes; feel it through some touch of truth to our own experience how the malignancy of the forces against us may be doubled by their uncertainty and the resultant confusion of one's own mind—blindfold night there, too, at the moment when daylight and self-possession are indispensable." So much purely in the interests of something else to come; the next sentence indicates a transition, after which we plunge into a further idea, fortified by the paragraph above:

"In that old dreamland of the *Iliad* such darkness is the work of a propitiable deity, and withdrawn at its pleasure;

in life, it often persists obstinately. It was so with the agents on the terrible Eve of St. Bartholomew, 1572, when a man's foes were those of his own household. An ambiguity of motive and influence, a confusion of spirit amounting, as we approach the center of action, to physical madness, encompasses those who are formally responsible for things; and the mist around that great crime, or great 'accident,' in which the gala weather of Gaston's coming to Paris broke up, leaving a sullenness behind it to remain for a generation, has never been penetrated. The doubt with which Charles the Ninth would seem to have left the world, doubt as to his own complicity therein, as well as to the precise nature, the course and scope, of the event itself, is still unresolved."

Gaston, however, has appeared by name in this second block; the theme now focuses itself on him entirely:

"So it was with Gaston also. The incident in his life which opened for him the profoundest sources of regret and pity, shaped as it was in a measure by those greater historic movements, owed its tragic significance there to an unfriendly shadow precluding knowledge how certain facts had gone, a shadow which veiled from others a particular act of his and the true character of its motives."

This is, however, merely the overture to the chapter, and is followed by a treatment of the same subjects in detail. Charles is examined more specifically—although here again with bare touches, the author never allowing himself to come to a complete rest—while Gaston's personal dilemma is interwoven. Significantly, the massacre itself, the subject of the chapter, is handled obliquely throughout, as vague smoke on the horizon, while we watch an old woman die of old age, with no knowledge of the butchery now going on in Paris, and "the light creeps over the silent cornfields, the last sense of it in those aged eyes now ebbing softly away."

This leisurely approach rests to a great extent on Pater's

idea of style. A subject was valuable to him in that it offered possibilities for a show of deftness. In *Marius the Epicurean* he has a scene of the somewhat godless court listening to an address by Fronto, an effulgent oratory in praise of the rigid Stoic doctrine; they sit about with their tablets ready to write down some especially happy phrasing, arranged comfortably among the images and flowers, and "ready to give themselves wholly to the intellectual treat prepared for them; applauding, blowing loud kisses through the air sometimes, at the speaker's triumphant exit from one of his long, skilfully modulated sentences." Pater's audience is expected to bring somewhat the same critical appreciation to bear, watching with keen pleasure as the artist extricates himself from the labyrinths of his material—a process which Pater loves so greatly that he often seems to make his labyrinths of his extrications. Art to Pater was "not the conveyance of an abstract body of truths," but "the critical tracing of . . . conscious artistic structure." He thought of a sentence as a happening—he prized particularly "the resolution of an obscure and complex idea into its component parts." He wrote fiction as though he were writing essays. Other men have sought the values of power and directness; Pater was interested, rather, in laying numerous angles of approach. Consequently, he wrote, to use his own term, as a scholar, interested vitally in the mechanism of his sentences, using words with an almost philological emphasis, "prescribing the rejection of many a neology, many a license, many a gipsy phrase which might present itself as actually expressive." His preference for artifice was consistent: "We shall not wish our boys to sing like mere birds," he says in the best *fin de siècle* accent. And he decides that the *Phædo* gives the true death of Socrates since "in the details of what there happened, the somewhat prosaic account of the way in which the work of death was done, we find what there could have been no literary satisfaction in inventing." It is harder to understand his complaint that "to Browne the whole world is a museum," or his untroubled aspersions upon "those lengthy leisurely terminations which busy posterity will abbreviate," for it is only by enjoying such qualities in Browne that we can forgive them in Pater. He likewise is characterizing himself when he speaks of Browne as being on the alert for surprises in nature "as if nature had a rhetoric," though Sir Thomas was far superior to Pater in disclosing it.

Poets, deciding that the world needs or does not need woman suffrage, or the forty-four-hour week, or being interested in how someone starts a traction company in Idaho, write accordingly. But Pater must take only such subjects as are "categorically" dignified, subjects in his case concerned with the culture and traditions of whole peoples. He manifested that philosophic—or perhaps, in the truest sense, cultured—turn of mind which finds the specific interesting only through its correlations with the general (the general with him usually bearing on the Mediterranean and its traditions, Hellenism, the growth of the Gothic, humanism, and the like). His heroes, therefore, will always exemplify in microcosm what their environment exemplifies in macrocosm; whole hordes are moving blindly as his lonely hero moves with an acutely circumspect consciousness.

As one of the deepest consequents of a nostalgia for tradition, came the development of a peculiar earthiness. This naturally turned him away from the Protestantism of his countrymen, who, with all their emphasis on the home, never developed equivalents to the Lares and Penates. A people more direct in its religion would divide and subdivide its divinities until they fitted one peculiar locality. The only man in England who had recaptured this feeling in all thoroughness was Wordsworth; and Pater admired him greatly. Wordsworth, however, had stopped with the abstract spirit of a place; he had left the outlines for some *numen,* some god of the locality. By a queer twist, what Wordsworth had done from living immediately against the soil, Pater was to understand and exemplify in his study at Oxford. Yet, characteristically, his interest in the spirit of the soil was not specific, like that of Wordsworth, but ideological. The attitude was a hothouse product: genuine but forced.

Having become saturated with his humanism, he carried it back as far as he could, which was to the earth. This attitude is seen at its finest in the opening chapters of *Marius the Epicurean,* where the hero starts with a dignity, a "sweetness," that is, so far as I know, unique in literature. The peculiar literary value lies in this early stabilization which is given to Marius, so that at the very beginning he is an entity, to be subtly dispersed later by the intricate conflicts of his times. His grave bewilderment in this mosaic work of ethics has a purer balance, superimposed as it is upon the soberness and placidity of the pastoral.

Ideology in Pater was used for its flavor of beauty, rather than of argument. He treated ideas not for their value as statements, but as horizons, situations, developments of plot, in short, as any other element of fiction. The reader who looks into *Marius the Epicurean* for an addition to Stoicism or Epicureanism will find nothing of value there; for the disclosures arise solely from the interplay of these two moralities, as they follow upon the spontaneous gods and are followed by Christianity.

Any number of people have been interested in the contemporary "transvaluation of values," and have written of it in some minutely particular application; it is perhaps the favored theme of the last half-century's novelists. But whereas many writers who sought the brightly new attained the mere superficialities of such transvaluing, Pater caught some of its deepest elements even while "prescribing the rejection of many a neology" and choosing subjects remote in history. In this one respect he may be linked with Nietzsche: both kept the theme of transvaluation well within the sphere of ceremony.

As Pater observes in his study of Plato, however, even Heraclitus, the philosopher of eternal change, the inventor of the dictum that "everything flows," seems in the end to have been searching for those changeless principles which might govern perpetual change. Similarly Pater follows to its conclusion his predilection for the fluctuant, and dwells in the vicinity of the Ens, the Immutable, the Absolute. But as an artist rather than a metaphysician, he was content to retain this Immutable solely for its contribution to his vocabulary of flux. The contemplation of permanent things served primarily to strengthen his depiction of the evanescent. Having thus a balance of thesis and antithesis, the issue demanded no further penetration on his part. He could content himself with drawing out the effects of his subject, aware that there was at least the indubitable and immediate certainty of his craft. And if, by the doctrines of his century, the dignity of man in nature had been prejudiced atrociously, the predicament meant hardly more to Pater than an added incentive to proclaim the dignity of man in art.

III

In his essay on women and language, De Gourmont comments on the tendency of the young males to burn up the race, and adds that certain Asiatic peoples are extinct not on account of their lack of spirit, but because they had too much of it. De Gourmont himself began his career at a time when one of the most feverish attempts in the history of European art was being made to burn up the race. The group of young males that gathered around Mallarmé, with their æsthetic of symbolism, and their philosophy of idealism, were, as

De Gourmont proudly showed in one of his early insolent polemics, on the road to intellectual anarchism. If each man was his own world—and surely, there are certain poems of Mallarmé which we can only spy at quizzically, as one might look through a 'scope at Venus under favorable conditions —it was inevitable that each man should have his own idiom. Although the reduction to absurdity of individualism in art is to spend one's life in talking to oneself, they were all too potent, too spirited, to be disturbed by reductions to absurdity. If such was the quintessence of symbolism, there was nothing to do but talk to oneself; the movement *per se* was its justification.

All this fever of innovation was decried under the name of decadence, though De Gourmont shows in his *Mallarmé et l'Idée de Décadence* that the historical concept of *décadisme* referred to times when the creative instinct was at its lowest, not at its suicidally highest.

To be a decadent, by another association of ideas, was to uphold the infamous *L'art-pour-l'art*. De Gourmont always had much too strong a detestation of democratic standards to be anything but a disciple of Art for Art's Sake. In *Une Nuit au Luxembourg* he says:

"The process of thinking is a sport, although this sport must be free and harmonious. The more it is looked upon as useless, the more one feels the need of making it beautiful. Beauty—that is perhaps its only possible value."

And in one of his essays:

"To admit art because it can uplift the masses or the individual, is like admitting the rose because we can extract from roses a medicine for the eyes."

Art was "justified" because art was an appetite—in being desired it found its ample reason for existence. Art did not require defense as an instrument of political or social reform. Art was purely and simply a privilege, to be prized as a cosmic exception. And far from trying to show that art "does good," De Gourmont would find art of primary value even if it "did harm." Art would naturally seem "subversive" if judged by non-art standards. Reversing the customary direction of approach, De Gourmont pointed out that intellectual pursuits alone distinguished man from other organisms—accordingly, instead of appraising these pursuits by their social usefulness, he would appraise our social institutions by their usefulness in making intellectual pursuits possible.

This attitude manifested itself in the experimental nature of both his critical and imaginative writings. His one imperative was to be venturesome. Since art, by becoming an end in itself, became a matter of the individual—or by becoming a matter of the individual, became an end in itself—he was theoretically without external obligations, at liberty to develop his medium as he preferred. And while this theoretical freedom was checked in him, as in every artist, by the desire to communicate, it did contribute to the variability of his work. It is true that he ceased his stylistic development once he had reached a complete lubrication of phrase, but the nature of his books themselves is rarely the same in two successive volumes. Against the opulence of *Sixtine,* with its baggage of erudite irony and rhetorical excursions, is the suave, almost unctuous *Une Nuit au Luxembourg.* There is the nearly conventional novel, *Un Cœur Virginal,* with complications, opportune disclosures, and the like; but there is also *Les Chevaux de Diomède,* "a little novel of possible adventures, with thought, action, dream, and sensuality treated on the same plane and analysed with equal good will." His fantastic stories, written when symbolism was in its first glow, are matched by things like the somewhat nasty *Histoires Magiques.* And scattered among this pliant fiction are his criticisms, grammatical writings, works of scientific research, philosophical essays, notes on contemporary society, discussions of art and literature, and an occasional poem—in all some forty volumes of graceful and intelligent writing. Were they not diffuse, there is no grave objection that could be laid against them.

In 1883, at the age of twenty-five, De Gourmont began his life in Paris as a man of letters. For about eight years he worked in the Bibliothèque Nationale, during which time he wrote some scientific articles of vulgarization; but in 1891 his connections with the library were suddenly brought to a close by his publication of an anti-chauvinistic article, *Le Joujou Patriotisme*. About this time also he suffered the beginnings of a malady which is alluded to but vaguely by his friends, but which kept him for the most of his life confined to his rooms in the Rue des Saints-Pères. This malady was leprosy. Surely there is no other case in history of a man who remained so "Olympian" in his speculations while secretly afflicted with a burden traditionally held so awesome. Only by negation can we discover his difficulties. The exceptional physical neatness of his women is perhaps the too-eager denial of his own disease. And the "illusion of liberty," which he formulated as the psychological counterpart to his theories of determinism, is perhaps to a degree a compensation for the serious strictures upon his actual way of living. But essentially he was too intelligent for cataclysm, too inquisitive for personal tragedy. Though his philosophy led him far from Flaubert's adulation of work, his productivity soon started a rumor in Parisian literary circles that Remy de Gourmont was a group of writers using one pseudonym. He remained until his death a man closed in his study, seen by a few intimates, living almost exclusively with books. Besides his knowledge of the standard names in philosophy and literature, his familiarity with late Latin opened up to him a great fund of mediæval misery and error, and many a volume which he frankly admired for its lubricity. For experience, he had his tomes; for vitality, the beating of his own veins. And for a slogan, perhaps a hysterical slogan, but thoroughly justified in his case, he had his "illusion of liberty," which might enable us to say of him what he said of France: *"un pays qui possède, avec l'Italie, la littérature la plus libre de l'Europe et la plus délicieusement érotique."*

Super-Copernican, De Gourmont was not content with denying the world as the center of the universe; he also denies man as the center of the world. He found in Darwin *"la pudibonderie religieuse de sa race,"* and the purely theological tendency, even while endangering the old religion, to place man as the ultimate aim of nature. He insisted that man was neither first nor last upon the earth. The privileges of humanity were hardly more than an accident, if one could speak of an accident in nature, and this accident might just as well have happened to another species, indeed, may still happen. Intelligence is perhaps an improper functioning of the instincts, or the beginning of instincts which have not yet crystallized—which would mean that the bee or the ant had gone further in evolution than man. In his *Physique de l'Amour,* he says, "Man is not at the pinnacle of nature; he is *in* nature, one of the units of life, and nothing more." The purpose of this book was to "place the sexual life of man in the one and only scheme of universal sexuality." De Gourmont never forgot that a man is of no more importance in relation to the stars than a grasshopper. Nor did he forget that a man in relation to himself is of tremendous importance. *"L'intelligence est un accident; le génie est une catastrophe,"* he wrote in *Le Succès et l'Idée de Beauté,* and the statement contained his highest possible tribute to intelligence and genius. De Gourmont found delight precisely where his predecessors had found despair.

While emphasizing the futility of the human race as a

whole, he affirmed the all-importance of the individual. Descartes' *cogito; ergo sum,* he says somewhere, is so simple, so rudimentary, that any savage could probably understand it. Humanity is an abstraction, but the isolated human has cravings to satisfy and pains to avoid; it is these exclusively personal experiences which are important so long as sensation endures. De Gourmont has little time for those perfect systems of government wherein the aggregate of humanity is to be made happy at the expense of each individual. "Let us accept as sufficient this theorem: What is useful to the bee is useful to the hive."

De Gourmont, with his insistence upon the unimportance of humanity and the importance of man, his conception of the intelligence as a disease or an error along with his enthusiasm over the beauty of a perfectly functioning intelligence, his balance of man as an animal over against man as something distinct from all animals, maintained a conflict of attitudes which gives his work considerable liquidity. Such ambivalence was characteristic. Thoroughly godless, for instance, he always manifested a passionate interest in Catholicism. His first important work of erudition, *Le Latin Mystique,* is an anthology, with partial translations and comment, of "the poets of the antiphonary, and Symbolism in the Middle Ages." His *Chemin de Velours* is an analysis of Pascal and the Jesuits. But, as one might expect, his sympathy for Catholicism is hardly likely to earn for him the benediction of Rome. For he admires Catholicism in that it is preserving the rich pagan institutions over against the aridity of Protestantism. Mere matters of creed mean nothing to him; like many of his pious colleagues, he is interested in the Church as a pageant. He observes with regret that before the Reformation the Church was steadily incorporating the elements of paganism; he shows the functions and names of Italian tutelary deities surviving as saints of the calendar; he points out that the Greek god Orpheus, who often figures in early Christian art, was accepted as a prophet by no less an authority than St. Augustine. "A pure Christianity would have rejected the entire Pythagorean system; Catholicism, true to its name, has handed down to us, along with the religion of Christ, nearly all the superstitions and all the theogonies of the Orient." It is not the Protestant Revolution which distresses De Gourmont, but the Catholic Reformation. From then on the existence of beauty in the Church has been precarious; Church art practically ceased; the Church had been Christianized.

"*Il y a un art catholique; il n'y a pas d'art chrétien; le christianisme évangélique est essentiellement opposé à toute représentation de la beauté sensible, soit d'après le corps humain, soit d'après le reste de la nature.*"

As an inevitable corollary to such an attitude towards the Church was De Gourmont's insistence upon the primacy of sex. (Although I do not recall his ever mentioning the name of a psychoanalyst—and he is always frank about his sources —the theories of Freud and his epigons are continually finding expression in his works. The parallelism is natural enough, however—for De Gourmont was the leading apologist of symbolism, and as Charles Baudouin has pointed out, psychoanalysis is the scientific counterpart of symbolist art.) "The mistake of treating man's brain as the absolute centre of the man is both fortunate and commendable, but it is a mistake. The only natural aim of man is that of reproduction." Or from another angle, "*La beauté est si bien sexuelle que les seules œuvres d'art incontestées sont celles qui montrent tout bonnement le corps humain dans sa nudité.* By its insistence on remaining purely sexual, Greek statuary has lifted itself forever above all discussion."

But all this is only one phase of his sympathy with the life of the senses. De Gourmont is even more thoroughly an

Epicurean than Anatole France. He says in *Le Chemin de Velours* that "Voluptuosity is a creation of man, a delicate art in which only a few are especially proficient, like music or painting." *Une Nuit au Luxembourg* contains a new apology for Epicurus:

"My friend, for some centuries now the schools have been poisoning your sensibilities and strangling your intelligence by making you believe that the pleasures of Epicurus were exclusively pleasures of the mind. Epicurus was too wise to disdain any sort of pleasure. He wanted to know, and he did know, all the satisfactions which can become the satisfactions of men; he abused nothing, but he used everything, in his life of harmony."

In the closing chapter of his *Physique de l'Amour* he has a long, enthusiastic period: *"Tout n'est que luxure. . . . L'animal ignore la diversité, l'accumulation des aptitudes; l'homme seul est luxurieux."* M. Paul Delior, in his *Remy de Gourmont et Son Œuvre*, illustrates the attitude of De Gourmont by citing the three souls of Plato: the νοῦς, "mind, intelligence," located in the head; the θῦμος, "passions, emotions," located in the breast; the ἐπιθυμήτικον, with all the appetites which assure the conservation of the individual and of the race, located in the stomach, and according to Plato a ferocious beast which we should nurture only because it is necessary to existence. De Gourmont not only admired the purest activities of the intellect, and the play of the sensibilities, but also recognized the dignity of the appetites, understood that they are an excellent base on which to erect the superstructure of intelligence and sensibility.

De Gourmont discovered himself for his critics when he used the word "dissociation." He loves to show that a concept which we generally take as a unit can be subdivided. "Man associates his ideas, not in accordance with logic, or verifiable exactitude, but in accordance with his desires and his interests." In his essay, *La Dissociation des Idées,* De Gourmont lets himself loose with this method, and produces a type of writing which is delightfully exact. After defining the origin of the commonplace, he gives as an example the association of ideas Byzantium–decadence. He then goes over to the nature of morality, and the reasonable probability that the individual can develop more conveniently in immorality; but morality is the determination to preserve the race at the expense of the individual. From this he comes to the association carnal pleasure–generation, as the foundation of sexual morality. Yet the true association, he holds, is that of intellectuality–infecundity. Christianity, however, did make one remarkable dissociation, that of love and carnal pleasure. Thus was the love of brother and sister made possible. I recall that in his *Octavius,* Minucius Felix found it necessary to refute the Roman scandal about the Christian "brotherly love." De Gourmont, as also Minucius, uses the instance of the Egyptians, who could not understand love without sexual conjunction. He next considers Joan of Arc, and the conflicting associations she brings up in an English and a French mind. Soon he has arrived at the army, showing how at one time the military was associated with high honor; then came scandals, and the mistake was just as radically the other way, the military becoming associated with nothing but complete dishonor. In closing he leaves us a list which he has not troubled to examine, but which seems to fall apart by the mere clarity of juxtaposition: virtue–recompense; wrong–punishment; God–goodness; crime–remorse; duty–happiness; future–progress. It is regrettable that De Gourmont did not carry his dissociative method further into the realm of literary criticism. The method was clearly a companion discovery to symbolism, which sought its effects precisely by utilizing, more programmatically than in any previous movement, the clusters of associations surrounding the important words of a poem or fiction. And such writers as James Joyce and Gertrude Stein are clearly making associative and dissociative processes a pivotal concern of their works. Any technical criticism of our methodological authors of today must concern itself with the further development and schematization of such ideas as De Gourmont was considering.

An author who lives most of his life in his head must perform his transgressions on paper. There was many a wild act more or less definitely spelled out in De Gourmont's ink. In his fiction, the graceful libertinage of the man is perhaps one of his predominant qualities. He seemed to prefer the contemplation of easy conquests, of women that were at once refined and ready of access, and men who were frankly satyrs. "Arise, thy name is Lilith," says Jehovah in creating pre-Eve woman. Lilith, arising, speaks: *"Donne-moi l'homme, Seigneur."* As a matter of course, Diomedes attains all women except Christine, and she is immune only because she does not exist. True, in *Sixtine,* D'Entragues is baffled, but it is his endless ratiocination that defeats him; and as recompense, this same ratiocination aids him in the last chapter to console himself, and reach *"le repos final,"* a mock-Victorian "In Conclusion." In *Un Cœur Virginal,* the leading character fails with the heroine because he is dangerously nearing his fifties, and De Gourmont is writing the physiology of virginity; it is part of the physiology that a younger man should win. With this one important exception, as he developed his method De Gourmont seemed to profit more and more by his "illusion of liberty," until in the *Lettres d'un Satyre* we have as hero a complete Olympian, who treats his women as flowers in the earlier Goethe fashion—*Röslein, Röslein, Röslein rot!*—and plucks them where he will.

Blasphemy is another element which recurs, blasphemy

and sacrilege. *Le Fantôme,* for instance, is a perverse account of a courtship which he has enwrapped in mysticism by utilizing the language of the ritual. It is a pagan plot made churchy, with a fictitious mass to celebrate the glory of love. However, in a personality as rich as that of De Gourmont, blasphemy can never be insolence or derision. It is often the expression of the religious inclination in an intelligence which cannot believe. Since it is impossible to praise the divinities with sincerity, there is nothing left but to insult them. Blasphemy is a serious experiment, a transgression by means of the sins of others. To blaspheme is to restore the lost gods by renouncing them; blasphemy is the struggle of an emotional nature, a protest against the intellect which tends to make it sterile of religious ecstasy. Blasphemy is impious, but it is not irreligious.

In his highly pietistic introduction to *Pendant la Guerre,* Jean de Gourmont finds that "in spite of the echo of the battle, and that atmosphere of anguish in which we were all plunged, the writer's hand had not trembled, nor his brain; never perhaps has Remy de Gourmont attained as in these few months such clarity of style and of thought stripped of all vain metaphor, all vain literature."

One was expected to write so during the war, but I doubt if any could still feel that the war had brought De Gourmont a greater "clarity of thought." For here, like poor Diomède of twenty years earlier, De Gourmont had at last slipped against life and been forced to suffer the overbalancing of his intellect by his emotions. A social force had appeared which was strong enough to break through his detachment, and as Diomède finally accepted the ideal of the sluggish Pascase, so De Gourmont half fell in with the universal licking of blood that for five years was supposed to be the purest expression of humanity.

Once he had written, "Detachment is the most aristocratic

of all aristocratic attitudes. .... We should take part in the game, and with pleasure, but not with passion. Passion disqualifies; it is the proof of an elementary organism, without serious co-ordination. ...."

"*Toutes les questions qui agitent les peuples, émeuvent les individus, acquièrent . . . l'importance du fétu qui révolutionne une formilière.*"

And again, in *La Création Subconsciente*, he remarks that a man loses his personality in acting sympathetically with a great number of people. Thus, De Gourmont himself has furnished us with reasons to distrust his blaze of patriotism. And whatever may be said in favor of a blaze of patriotism, we have it on his own authority that it can hardly be admired as an aid to greater clarity of style and thought.

No, De Gourmont was now cast against life for the first time. The war had startled him out of his theory, deprived him of the purity of his Epicureanism. The vigor of his intelligence, it seems, had delayed as far as old age the struggle with vital forces that most of us have experienced before twenty. Until now, he had succeeded in saddling his emotions with ideas; but the war, which was hardly more than an irritation to so many, became to him overwhelming. For the most part, his war books are the magnificent ruins of a great intelligence. Suddenly De Gourmont needed his god; and since the godlessness of his youth was freedom, his god became attachment. He retained his keenness, and in most cases his leisure, but the full force of the war, the threat that France might be destroyed, called for affirmation, for patriotic dogmatizing. De Gourmont, joining the swarm *pour la patrie*, trained his learned barrage upon the barbarians. The spirit of irony, of contradiction, of impersonality, that ultimate flavor of his versatility which made him an exquisite writer, had dropped away. As he says of himself, his ideas were mobilized.

But even the ruins of De Gourmont are of no ordinary nature. Never, during the entire war, did he degenerate to the level of a war editorial. He is not among those who would decry Nietzsche, for he recognized that Nietzsche was one of the most important moralists of the time; and further, there is Nietzsche in every sentence he wrote. He admitted the value of German music. He managed to keep reasonably clean of the "regeneration" mud, the thesis which became the reason for existence of half the output of the novel-manufacturing industry of England, the song that the war must create a profound uplift in everyone. But essentially he accepted the formula: that the enemy was *always* wrong. He seemed to have forgotten his own dissociative method, he was so busy helping to nourish the association, enemy-turpitude.

Perhaps De Gourmont could no longer contradict, but he could modify. He recognized that the basis of this war, as of every war, was the pugnacity natural to all individual or collective egos. Even the enemy's "atrocities" he sometimes defended as a corollary of the war-spirit. He blamed the war on militarism, although militarism to De Gourmont was not a term in economics; De Gourmont could always talk more enthusiastically of man in comparison with his analysis of a sea mollusk than he could from consideration of the industrial revolution. Essentially, the present war for him, aside from the painful fact that it was his own personal friends who were dying, was not different from an unwritten event of pre-history, a struggle with clubs.

In *Une Nuit au Luxembourg,* where "Lui" is considering the destruction of the human race, he dismisses the thought of some great cataclysm like an explosion or like collision with a comet, not because it is improbable, but because it is too crude, too broadly theatrical, to interest him. The development of De Gourmont's writing during the war indicates that if he had lived, the war might have suffered the same fate with him. Gradually the brooding quality of his early notes on the war disappears; he becomes more and more discursive, with more emphasis on the theoretical and observational, the essentially egotistic. He is in the war much the way one would be on the sea or in the mountains; since it is the most prevailing fact, he talks about it.

In *La Culture des Idées* he had written, *"La diabolique Intelligence rit des exorcismes, et l'eau bénite de l'Université n'a jamais pu la stériliser, non plus que celle de l'Eglise."* And he might have added, *"ou de la guerre,"* for at the time of his death, only a little more than a year after the beginning of hostilities, he was planning *La Physique des Mœurs,* a book entirely free of the war.

PSYCHOLOGY AND FORM

IT is not until the fourth scene of the first act that Hamlet confronts the ghost of his father. As soon as the situation has been made clear, the audience has been, consciously or unconsciously, waiting for this ghost to appear, while in the fourth scene this moment has been definitely promised. For earlier in the play Hamlet had arranged to come to the platform at night with Horatio to meet the ghost, and it is now night, he is with Horatio and Marcellus, and they are standing on the platform. Hamlet asks Horatio the hour.

> "Hor. I think it lacks of twelve.
> Mar. No, it is struck.
> Hor. Indeed? I heard it not: then it draws near the season
>   Wherein the spirit held his wont to walk."

Promptly hereafter there is a sound off-stage. "A flourish of trumpets, and ordnance shot off within." Hamlet's friends have established the hour as twelve. It is time for the ghost. Sounds off-stage, and of course it is not the ghost. It is, rather, the sound of the king's carousal, for the king "keeps wassail." A tricky, and useful, detail. We have been waiting for a ghost, and get, startlingly, a blare of trumpets. And, once the trumpets are silent, we feel how desolate are these three men waiting for a ghost, on a bare "platform," feel it by this sudden juxtaposition of an imagined scene of lights and merriment. But the trumpets announcing a carousal have suggested a subject of conversation. In the darkness Hamlet discusses the excessive drinking of his countrymen.

He points out that it tends to harm their reputation abroad, since, he argues, this one showy vice makes their virtues "in the general censure take corruption." And for this reason, although he himself is a native of this place, he does not approve of the custom. Indeed, there in the gloom he is talking very intelligently on these matters, and Horatio answers, "Look, my Lord, it comes." All this time we had been waiting for a ghost, and it comes at the one moment which was not pointing towards it. This ghost, so assiduously prepared for, is yet a surprise. And now that the ghost has come, we are waiting for something further. Program: a speech from Hamlet. Hamlet must confront the ghost. Here again Shakespeare can feed well upon the use of contrast for his effects. Hamlet has just been talking in a sober, rather argumentative manner—but now the flood-gates are unloosed:

"Angels and ministers of grace defend us!
Be thou a spirit of health or goblin damn'd,
Bring with thee airs from heaven or blasts from hell . . ."

and the transition from the matter-of-fact to the grandiose, the full-throated and full-voweled, is a second burst of trumpets, perhaps even more effective than the first, since it is the rich fulfilment of a promise. Yet this satisfaction in turn becomes an allurement, an itch for further developments. At first desiring solely to see Hamlet confront the ghost, we now want Hamlet to learn from the ghost the details of the murder—which are, however, with shrewdness and husbandry, reserved for "Scene V.—Another Part of the Platform."

I have gone into this scene at some length, since it illustrates so perfectly the relationship between psychology and form, and so aptly indicates how the one is to be defined in terms of the other. That is, the psychology here is not the psychology of the *hero,* but the psychology of the *audience.* And by that distinction, form would be the psychology of the audience. Or, seen from another angle, form is the creation of an appetite in the mind of the auditor, and the adequate satisfying of that appetite. This satisfaction—so complicated is the human mechanism—at times involves a temporary set of frustrations, but in the end these frustrations prove to be simply a more involved kind of satisfaction, and furthermore serve to make the satisfaction of fulfilment more intense. If, in a work of art, the poet says something, let us say, about a meeting, writes in such a way that we desire to observe that meeting, and then, if he places that meeting before us—that is form. While obviously, that is also the psychology of the audience, since it involves desires and their appeasements.

The seeming breach between form and subject-matter, between technique and psychology, which has taken place in the last century is the result, it seems to me, of scientific criteria being unconsciously introduced into matters of purely æsthetic judgment. The flourishing of science has been so vigorous that we have not yet had time to make a spiritual readjustment adequate to the changes in our resources of material and knowledge. There are disorders of the social system which are caused solely by our undigested wealth (the basic disorder being, perhaps, the phenomenon of over-production: to remedy this, instead of having all workers employed on half time, we have half working full time and the other half idle, so that whereas overproduction could be the greatest reward of applied science, it has been, up to now, the most menacing condition our modern civilization has had to face). It would be absurd to suppose that such social disorders would not be paralleled by disorders of culture and taste, especially since science is so pronouncedly a spiritual factor. So that we are, owing to the sudden wealth science has thrown upon us, all *nouveaux-riches* in matters of culture, and most poignantly in that field where lack of native firmness is most readily exposed, in matters of æsthetic judgment.

One of the most striking derangements of taste which science has temporarily thrown upon us involves the understanding of psychology in art. Psychology has become a body of information (which is precisely what psychology in science should be, or must be). And similarly, in art, we tend to look for psychology as the purveying of information. Thus, a contemporary writer has objected to Joyce's *Ulysses* on the ground that there are more psychoanalytic data available in Freud. (How much more drastically he might, by the same system, have destroyed Homer's *Odyssey!*) To his objection it was answered that one might, similarly, denounce Cézanne's trees in favor of state forestry bulletins. Yet are not Cézanne's landscapes themselves tainted with the psychology of information? Has he not, by perception, *pointed out* how one object lies against another, *indicated* what takes place between two colors (which is the psychology of science, and is less successful in the medium of art than in that of science, since in art such processes are at best implicit, whereas in science they are so readily made explicit)? Is Cézanne not, to that extent, a state forestry bulletin, except that he tells what goes on in the eye instead of on the tree? And do not the true values of his work lie elsewhere—and precisely in what I distinguish as the psychology of form?

Thus, the great influx of information has led the artist also to lay his emphasis on the giving of information—with the result that art tends more and more to substitute the psychology of the hero (the subject) for the psychology of the audience. Under such an attitude, when form is preserved it is preserved as an annex, a luxury, or, as some feel, a downright affectation. It remains, though sluggish, like the human appendix, for occasional demands are still made upon it; but its true vigor is gone, since it is no longer organically required. Proposition: The hypertrophy of the psychology of information is accompanied by the corresponding atrophy of the psychology of form.

In information, the matter is intrinsically interesting. And by intrinsically interesting I do not necessarily mean intrinsically valuable, as witness the intrinsic interest of backyard gossip or the most casual newspaper items. In art, at least the art of the great ages (Æschylus, Shakespeare, Racine) the matter is interesting by means of an extrinsic use, a function. Consider, for instance, the speech of Mark Antony, the "Brutus is an honourable man." Imagine in the same place a very competently developed thesis on human conduct, with statistics, intelligence tests, definitions; imagine it as the finest thing of the sort ever written, and as really being at the roots of an understanding of Brutus. Obviously, the play would simply stop until Antony had finished. For in the case of Antony's speech, the value lies in the fact that his words are shaping the future of the audience's desires, not the desires of the Roman populace, but the desires of the pit. This is the psychology of form as distinguished from the psychology of information.

The distinction is, of course, absolutely true only in its non-existent extremes. Hamlet's advice to the players, for instance, has little of the quality which distinguishes Antony's speech. It is, rather, intrinsically interesting, although one could very easily prove how the play would benefit by some such delay at this point, and that anything which made this delay possible without violating the consistency of the subject would have, in this, its formal justification. It would, furthermore, be absurd to rule intrinsic interest out

33

of literature. I wish simply to have it restored to its properly minor position, seen as merely one out of many possible elements of style. Goethe's prose, often poorly imagined, or neutral, in its line-for-line texture, especially in the treatment of romantic episode—perhaps he felt that the romantic episode in itself was enough?—is strengthened into a style possessing affirmative virtues by his rich use of aphorism. But this is, after all, but one of many possible facets of appeal. In some places, notably in *Wilhelm Meister's Lehrjahre* when Wilhelm's friends disclose the documents they have been collecting about his life unbeknown to him, the aphorisms are almost rousing in their efficacy, since they involve the story. But as a rule the appeal of aphorism is intrinsic: that is, it satisfies without being functionally related to the context.[1] . . . Also, to return to the matter of Hamlet, it must be observed that the style in this passage is no mere "information-giving" style; in its alacrity, its development, it really makes this one fragment into a kind of miniature plot.

One reason why music can stand repetition so much more sturdily than correspondingly good prose is that music, of all the arts, is by its nature least suited to the psychology of information, and has remained closer to the psychology of form. Here form cannot atrophy. Every dissonant chord cries for its solution, and whether the musician resolves or refuses to resolve this dissonance into the chord which the body cries for, he is dealing in human appetites. Correspondingly good prose, however, more prone to the temptations

---

[1] Similarly, the epigram of Racine is "pure art," because it usually serves to formulate or clarify some situation within the play itself. In Goethe the epigram is most often of independent validity, as in *Die Wahlverwandtschaften*, where the ideas of Ottilie's diary are obviously carried over bodily from the author's notebook. In Shakespeare we have the union of extrinsic and intrinsic epigram, the epigram growing out of its context and yet valuable independent of its context.

of pure information, cannot so much bear repetition since the æsthetic value of information is lost once that information is imparted. If one returns to such a work again it is purely because, in the chaos of modern life, he has been able to forget it. With a desire, on the other hand, its recovery is as agreeable as its discovery. One can memorize the dialogue between Hamlet and Guildenstern, where Hamlet gives Guildenstern the pipe to play on. For, once the speech is known, its repetition adds a new element to compensate for the loss of novelty. We cannot take a recurrent pleasure in the new (in information) but we can in the natural (in form). Already, at the moment when Hamlet is holding out the pipe to Guildenstern and asking him to play upon it, we "gloat over" Hamlet's triumphal descent upon Guildenstern, when, after Guildenstern has, under increasing embarrassment, protested three times that he cannot play the instrument, Hamlet launches the retort for which all this was preparation:

"Why, look you now, how unworthy a thing you make of me. You would play upon me, you would seem to know my stops; you would pluck out the heart of my mystery; you would sound me from my lowest note to the top of my compass; and there is much music, excellent voice, in this little organ, yet cannot you make it speak. 'Sblood, do you think I am easier to be played on than a pipe? Call me what instrument you will, though you can fret me, you cannot play upon me."[2]

In the opening lines we hear the promise of the close, and thus feel the emotional curve even more keenly than at first

---

[2] One might indicate still further appropriateness here. As Hamlet finishes his speech, Polonius enters, and Hamlet turns to him, "God bless you, sir!" Thus, the plot is continued (for Polonius is always the promise of action) and a full stop is avoided: the embarrassment laid upon Rosencranz and Guildenstern is not laid upon the audience.

reading. Whereas in most modern art this element is under-emphasized. It gives us the gossip of a plot, a plot which too often has for its value the mere fact that we do not know its outcome.[8]

Music, then, fitted less than any other art for imparting information, deals minutely in frustrations and fulfilments of desire,[4] and for that reason more often gives us those curves of emotion which, because they are natural, can bear repetition without loss. It is for this reason that music, like folk tales, is most capable of lulling us to sleep. A lullaby is a melody which comes quickly to rest, where the obstacles are easily overcome—and this is precisely the parallel to those waking dreams of struggle and conquest which (especially during childhood) we permit ourselves when falling asleep or when trying to induce sleep. Folk tales are just such waking dreams. Thus it is right that art should be called a "waking dream." The only difficulty with this definition (indicated by Charles Baudouin in his *Psychoanalysis and Æsthetics,* a very valuable study of Verhaeren) is that today we understand it to mean art as a waking dream for the artist. Modern criticism, and psychoanalysis in particular, is too prone to define the essence of art in terms of the artist's weaknesses. It is, rather, the audience which dreams, while the artist oversees the conditions which determine this dream. He is the manipulator of blood, brains, heart, and bowels which, while we sleep, dictate the mould of our

[8] Yet modern music has gone far in the attempt to renounce this aspect of itself. Its dissonances become static, demanding no particular resolution. And whereas an unfinished modulation by a classic musician occasions positive dissatisfaction, the refusal to resolve a dissonance in modern music does not dissatisfy us, but irritates or stimulates. Thus, "energy" takes the place of style.

[4] Suspense is the least complex kind of anticipation, as surprise is the least complex kind of fulfilment.

desires. This is, of course, the real meaning of artistic felicity
—an exaltation at the correctness of the procedure, so that we
enjoy the steady march of doom in a Racinian tragedy with
exactly the same equipment as that which produces our
delight with Benedick's "Peace! I'll stop your mouth. (*Kisses
her*)" which terminates the imbroglio of *Much Ado About
Nothing*.

The methods of maintaining interest which are most
natural to the psychology of information (as it is applied to
works of pure art) are surprise and suspense. The method
most natural to the psychology of form is eloquence. For
this reason the great ages of Æschylus, Shakespeare, and
Racine, dealing as they did with material which was more
or less a matter of common knowledge so that the broad
outlines of the plot were known in advance (while it is the
broad outlines which are usually exploited to secure surprise
and suspense) developed formal excellence, or eloquence, as
the basis of appeal in their work.

Not that there is any difference in kind between the classic
method and the method of the cheapest contemporary melodrama. The drama, more than any other form, must never
lose sight of its audience: here the failure to satisfy the
proper requirements is most disastrous. And since certain
contemporary work is successful, it follows that rudimentary
laws of composition are being complied with. The distinction is one of intensity rather than of kind. The contemporary audience hears the lines of a play or novel with the
same equipment as it brings to reading the lines of its daily
paper. It is content to have facts placed before it in some
more or less adequate sequence. Eloquence is the minimiz-
ing of this interest in fact, *per se,* so that the "more or less
adequate sequence" of their presentation must be relied on
to a much greater extent. Thus, those elements of surprise
and suspense are subtilized, carried down into the writing of

a line or a sentence, until in all its smallest details the work bristles with disclosures, contrasts, restatements with a difference, ellipses, images, aphorism, volume, sound-values, in short all that complex wealth of minutiæ which in their line-for-line aspect we call style and in their broader outlines we call form.

As a striking instance of a modern play with potentialities in which the intensity of eloquence is missing, I might cite a recent success, Capek's *R.U.R.* Here, in a melodrama which was often astonishing in the rightness of its technical procedure, when the author was finished he had written nothing but the scenario for a play by Shakespeare. It was a play in which the author produced time and again the opportunity, the demand, for eloquence, only to move on. (At other times, the most successful moments, he utilized the modern discovery of silence, with moments wherein words could not possibly serve but to detract from the effect: this we might call the "flowering" of information.) The Adam and Eve scene of the last act, a "commission" which the Shakespeare of the comedies would have loved to fill, was in the verbal barrenness of Capek's play something shameless to the point of blushing. The Robot, turned human, prompted by the dawn of love to see his first sunrise, or hear the first bird-call, and forced merely to say "Oh, see the sunrise," or "Hear the pretty birds"—here one could do nothing but wring his hands at the absence of that æsthetic mould which produced the overslung "speeches" of Romeo and Juliet.

Suspense is the concern over the possible outcome of some specific detail of plot rather than for general qualities. Thus, "Will A marry B or C?" is suspense. In *Macbeth*, the turn from the murder scene to the porter scene is a much less literal channel of development. Here the presence of one quality calls forth the demand for another, rather than one tangible incident of plot awaking an interest in some other possible tangible incident of plot. To illustrate more fully, if an author managed over a certain number of his pages to produce a feeling of sultriness, or oppression, in the reader, this would unconsciously awaken in the reader the desire for a cold, fresh northwind—and thus some aspect of a northwind would be effective if called forth by some aspect of stuffiness. A good example of this is to be found in a contemporary poem, T. S. Eliot's *The Waste Land,* where the vulgar, oppressively trivial conversation in the public house calls forth in the poet a memory of a line from Shakespeare. These slobs in a public house, after a desolately low-visioned conversation, are now forced by closing time to leave the saloon. They say good-night. And suddenly the poet, feeling his release, drops into another good-night, a good-night with *désinvolture,* a good-night out of what was, within the conditions of the poem at least, a graceful and irrecoverable past.

> "Well that Sunday Albert was home, they had a hot
> gammon,
> And they asked me in to dinner, to get the beauty of it
> hot"—[at this point the bartender interrupts: it is
> closing time]
> "Goonight Bill. Goonight Lou. Goonight May. Goonight.
> Ta ta. Goonight. Goonight.
> Good-night, ladies, good-night, sweet ladies, good-night,
> good-night."

There is much more to be said on these lines, which I have shortened somewhat in quotation to make my issue clearer. But I simply wish to point out here that this transition is a bold juxtaposition of one quality created by another, an association in ideas which, if not logical, is nevertheless emotionally natural. In the case of *Macbeth,* similarly, it would be absurd to say that the audience, after the murder scene, wants a porter scene. But the audience does want the quality which this porter particularizes. The dramatist might, conceivably, have introduced some entirely different character or event in this place, provided only that the event produced the same quality of relationship and contrast (grotesque seriousness followed by grotesque buffoonery). . . . One of the most beautiful and satisfactory "forms" of this sort is to be found in Baudelaire's *Femmes Damnées,* where the poet, after describing the business of a Lesbian seduction, turns to the full oratory of his apostrophe:

> *"Descendez, descendez, lamentables victimes,*
> *Descendez le chemin de l'enfer éternel . . ."*

while the stylistic efficacy of this transition contains a richness which transcends all moral (or unmoral) sophistication: the efficacy of appropriateness, of exactly the natural curve in treatment. Here is morality even for the godless, since it is a morality of art, being justified, if for no other reason, by its paralleling of that staleness, that disquieting loss of purpose, which must have followed the procedure of the two characters, the *femmes damnées* themselves, a remorse which, perhaps only physical in its origin, nevertheless becomes psychic.[5]

But to return, we have made three terms synonymous: form, psychology, and eloquence. And eloquence thereby becomes the essence of art, while pity, tragedy, sweetness, humor, in short all the emotions which we experience in life proper, as non-artists, are simply the material on which

---

[5] As another aspect of the same subject, I could cite many examples from the fairy tale. Consider, for instance, when the hero is to spend the night in a bewitched castle. Obviously, as darkness descends, weird adventures must befall him. His bed rides him through the castle; two halves of a man challenge him to a game of nine-pins played with thigh bones and skulls. Or entirely different incidents may serve instead of these. The quality comes first, the particularization follows.

eloquence may feed. The arousing of pity, for instance, is not the central purpose of art, although it may be an adjunct of artistic effectiveness. One can feel pity much more keenly at the sight of some actual misfortune—and it would be a great mistake to see art merely as a weak representation of some actual experience.[6] That artists today are content to write under such an æsthetic accounts in part for the inferior position which art holds in the community. Art, at least in the great periods when it has flowered, was the conversion, or transcendence, of emotion into eloquence, and was thus a factor added to life. I am reminded of St. Augustine's caricature of the theatre: that whereas we do not dare to wish people unhappy, we do want to feel sorry for them, and therefore turn to plays so that we can feel sorry although no real misery is involved. One might apply the parallel interpretation to the modern delight in happy endings, and say that we turn to art to indulge our humanitarianism in a well-wishing which we do not permit ourselves towards our actual neighbors. Surely the catharsis of art is more complicated than this, and more reputable.

Aren't endings happy wishing well towards ourselves

Eloquence itself, as I hope to have established in the instance from *Hamlet* which I have analyzed, is no mere plaster added to a framework of more stable qualities. Eloquence is simply the end of art, and is thus its essence. Even the poorest art is eloquent, but in a poor way, with less intensity, until this aspect is obscured by others fattening upon its leanness. Eloquence is not showiness; it is, rather, the result of that desire in the artist to make a work perfect by adapting it in every minute detail to the racial appetites.

[6] Could not the Greek public's resistance to Euripides be accounted for in the fact that he, of the three great writers of Greek tragedy, betrayed his art, was guilty of æsthetic impiety, in that he paid more attention to the arousing of emotion *per se* than to the sublimation of emotion into eloquence?

The distinction between the psychology of information and the psychology of form involves a definition of æsthetic truth. It is here precisely, to combat the deflection which the strength of science has caused to our tastes, that we must examine the essential breach between scientific and artistic truth. Truth in art is not the discovery of facts, not an addition to human knowledge in the scientific sense of the word.[7] It is, rather, the exercise of human propriety, the formulation of symbols which rigidify our sense of poise and rhythm. Artistic truth is the externalization of taste.[8] I sometimes wonder, for instance, whether the "artificial"

[7] One of the most striking examples of the encroachment of scientific truth into art is the doctrine of "truth by distortion," whereby one aspect of an object is suppressed the better to emphasize some other aspect; this is, obviously, an attempt to *indicate* by art some fact of knowledge, to make some implicit aspect of an object as explicit as one can by means of the comparatively dumb method of art (dumb, that is, as compared to the perfect ease with which science can indicate its discoveries). Yet science has already made discoveries in the realm of this "factual truth," this "truth by distortion" which must put to shame any artist who relies on such matter for his effects. Consider, for instance, the motion picture of a man vaulting. By photographing this process very rapidly, and running the reel very slowly, one has upon the screen the most striking set of factual truths to aid in our understanding of an athlete vaulting. Here, at our leisure, we can observe the contortions of four legs, a head and a butt. This squirming thing we saw upon the screen showed up an infinity of factual truths anent the balances of an athlete vaulting. We can, from this, observe the marvelous system of balancing which the body provides for itself in the adjustments of movement. Yet, so far as the æsthetic truth is concerned, this on the screen was not an athlete, but a squirming thing, a horror, displaying every fact of vaulting except the exhilaration of the act itself.

[8] The procedure of science involves the elimination of taste, employing as a substitute the corrective norm of the pragmatic test, the empirical experiment, which is entirely intellectual. Those who oppose the "intellectualism" of critics like Matthew Arnold are involved in an hilarious blunder, for Arnold's entire approach to the appreciation of art is through delicacies of taste intensified to the extent almost of squeamishness.

speech of John Lyly might perhaps be "truer" than the revelations of Dostoevsky. Certainly at its best, in its feeling for a statement which returns upon itself, which attempts the systole to a diastole, it *could* be much truer than Dostoevsky.[9] And if it is not, it fails not through a mistake of Lyly's æsthetic, but because Lyly was a man poor in character, whereas Dostoevsky was rich and complex. When Swift, making the women of Brobdingnag enormous, deduces from this discrepancy between their size and Gulliver's that Gulliver could sit astride their nipples, he has written something which is æsthetically true, which is, if I may be pardoned, profoundly "proper," as correct in its Euclidean deduction as any corollary in geometry. Given the companions of Ulysses in the cave of Polyphemus, it is true that they would escape clinging to the bellies of the herd let out to pasture. St. Ambrose, detailing the habits of God's creatures, and drawing from them moral maxims for the good of mankind, St. Ambrose in his limping natural history rich in scientific inaccuracies that are at the very heart of emotional rightness, St. Ambrose writes "Of night-birds, especially of the nightingale which hatches her eggs by song; of the owl, the bat, and the cock at cock-crow; in what wise these may apply to the guidance of our habits," and in the sheer rightness of that program there is the truth of art.

In introducing this talk of night-birds, after many pages devoted to other of God's creatures, he says,

"What now! While we have been talking, you will notice how the birds of night have already started fluttering about you, and, in this same fact of warning us to leave off with our discussion, suggest thereby a further topic"—and this seems to me to contain the best wisdom of which the human

---

[9] As for instance, the "conceit" of Endymion's awakening, when he forgets his own name, yet recalls that of his beloved.

frame is capable, an address, a discourse, which can make our material life seem blatant almost to the point of despair. And when the cock crows, and the thief abandons his traps, and the sun lights up, and we are in every way called back to God by the well-meaning admonition of this bird, here the very blindnesses of religion become the deepest truths of art.

THE POETIC PROCESS

IF WE WISH to indicate a gradual rise to a crisis, and speak of this as a climax, or a crescendo, we are talking in intellectualistic terms of a mechanism which can often be highly emotive. There is in reality no such general thing as a crescendo. What does exist is a multiplicity of individual art-works each of which may be arranged as a whole, or in some parts, in a manner which we distinguish as climactic. And there is also in the human brain the potentiality for reacting favorably to such a climactic arrangement. Over and over again in the history of art, different material has been arranged to embody the principle of the crescendo; and this must be so because we "think" in a crescendo, because it parallels certain psychic and physical processes which are at the roots of our experience. The accelerated motion of a falling body, the cycle of a storm, the procedure of the sexual act, the ripening of crops— growth here is not merely a linear progression, but a fruition. Indeed, natural processes are, inevitably, "formally" correct, and by merely recording the symptoms of some physical development we can obtain an artistic development. Thomas Mann's work has many such natural forms converted into art forms, as, in *Death in Venice,* his charting of a sunrise and of the progressive stages in a cholera epidemic. And surely, we may say without much fear of startling anyone, that the work of art utilizes climactic arrangement because the human brain has a pronounced potentiality for being arrested, or entertained, by such an arrangement.

But the concept "crescendo" does not have the emotive value of a crescendo. To arouse the human potentiality for being moved by the crescendo, I must produce some particular experience embodying a crescendo, a story, say, about A and B, where A becomes more and more involved in difficulties with B and finally shoots him. Here I have replaced the concept by a work of art illustrating it, and now for the first time I have an opportunity of making the crescendo play upon the human emotions.

In this way the work of art is seen to involve a principle of individuation. A shoots B in a crescendo, X weathers a flood and rescues Y in a crescendo—the artist may particularize, or individuate, the crescendo in any of the myriad aspects possible to human experience, localizing or channelizing it according to the chance details of his own life and vision. And similarly, throughout the permutations of history, art has always appealed, by the changing individuations of changing subject-matter, to certain potentialities of appreciation which would seem to be inherent in the very germ-plasm of man, and which, since they are constant, we might call innate forms of the mind. These forms are the "potentiality for being interested by certain processes or arrangements," or the "feeling for such arrangements of subject-matter as produce crescendo, contrast, comparison, balance, repetition, disclosure, reversal, contraction, expansion, magnification, series, and so on." Such "forms of the mind" might be listed at greater length. But I shall stop at the ones given, as I believe they illustrate to the extent of being a definition of my meaning. At bottom these "forms" may be looked upon as minor divisions of the two major "forms," unity and diversity. In any case, both unity and diversity will be found intermingling in any example of such forms. Contrast, for instance, is the use of elements which conflict in themselves but are both allied to a broader unity (as laughter on one page, tears on the next, but each involving an incident which furthers the growth of the plot). But the emotions cannot enjoy these forms, or laws (naturally, since they are merely the *conditions of emotional response*) except in their concreteness, in their quasi-vitiating material incorporation, in their specification or individuation.

This statement can be made clearer by comparing and contrasting it with the doctrines of Plato. Plato taught that the world of our senses is the manifestation of divine law through material. Thus, he supposed certain archetypes, or pure ideas, existing in heaven, while the objects of sensuous experience were good, true, and beautiful in proportion as they exemplified the pure form or idea behind them. Physical, or sensuous beauty, is valuable in so far as it gives us glimpses of the divine beauty, the original form, of which it is an imperfect replica.

Scholastic philosophy concerned itself principally with the problems raised by this teaching. The divine forms were called universals, and the concept of a principle of individuation was employed to describe the conditions under which we could experience these divine forms. *"Universale intelligitur, singulare sentitur,"* their position was finally stated: "We think in terms of universals, but we feel particulars." Or, to illustrate, "We may make an intellectual concept of goodness, but we can experience only some particular good thing."

Thus, the Platonic teaching was gradually reversed, and finally became branded as representative of a typically erroneous attitude. To say that an object is good in that it reflects the divine idea, or archetype, of goodness is, according to the nominalists, the mistake of hypostatization, of mistaking a linguistic convenience for a metaphysical reality. What really happens, they say, is that we find certain objects appealing in one way or another (tasty, beneficial, mild, obedient) and in the economy of speech use the word "good" for all these aspects of appeal. And since another economy of speech is the conversion of adjectives into nouns, we next turn "good"

47

into "goodness" and suppose that there is some actual thing, sitting somewhere, which corresponds to this word. This is to misunderstand the nature of language, they assert: and this misunderstanding results from the naïve supposition that, since each object has a word to designate it, so each word designates an object. Thus, they see no need for going from the particular to the universal; and they might, rather, define goodness as a complex of conditions in the human mind, body, and environment which make some objects, through a variety of ways, more appealing than others.

So eager were the nominalists to disavow Plato in detail, that they failed to discover the justice of his doctrines in essence. For we need but take his universals out of heaven and situate them in the human mind (a process begun by Kant), making them not metaphysical, but psychological. Instead of divine forms, we now have "conditions of appeal." There need not be a "divine contrast" in heaven for me to appreciate a contrast; but there *must be* in my mind the sense of contrast. The researches of anthropologists indicate that man has "progressed" in cultural cycles which repeat themselves in essence (in form) despite the limitless variety of specific details to embody such essences, or forms. Speech, material traits (for instance, tools), art, mythology, religion, social systems, property, government, and war—these are the nine "potentials" which man continually re-individuates into specific cultural channels, and which anthropologists call the "universal pattern." And when we speak of psychological universals, we mean simply that just as there is inborn in the germ-plasm of a dog the potentiality of barking, so there is inborn in the germ-plasm of man the potentiality of speech, art, mythology, and so on. And while these potentialities are continually changing their external aspects, their "individuations," they do not change in essence. Given the potentiality for speech, the child of any culture will speak the language which it hears. There is no mental equipment for speaking Chinese which is different from the mental equipment for speaking English. But the potentiality externalizes itself in accordance with the traditions into which the individual happens to be born. And by education we do not mean the "awaking" of a moral, or religious, or social, or artistic sense, but the leading of such potentialities into one specific channel. We cannot teach the moral sense any more than we can teach abstract thought to a dog. But we can individuate the moral sense by directing it into a specific code or tradition. The socialists today imply this fact when they object to the standard *bourgeois* education, meaning that it channelizes the potentialities of the child into a code which protects the *bourgeois* interests, whereas they would have these same potentialities differently individuated to favor the proletarian revolution.

This, I hope, should be sufficient to indicate that there is no hypostatization in speaking of innate forms of the mind, and mentioning "laws" which the work of art makes accessible to our emotions by individuation. And for our purposes we might translate the formula *"universale intelligitur, singulare sentitur"* into some such expansion as this: "We can discuss the basic forms of the human mind under such concepts as crescendo, contrast, comparison, and so on. But to experience them emotionally, we must have them singularized into an example, an example which will be chosen by the artist from among his emotional and environmental experiences."

Whereupon, returning to the Poetic Process, let us suppose that while a person is sleeping some disorder of the digestion takes place, and he is physically depressed. Such depression in the sleeper immediately calls forth a corresponding psychic depression, while this psychic depression in turn translates itself into the invention of details which will more or less adequately symbolize this depression. If the sleeper has had some set of experiences strongly marked by the feeling of depression, his mind may summon details from this experience to symbolize his depression. If he fears financial ruin, his depression may very reasonably seize upon the cluster of facts associated with this fear in which to individuate itself. On the other hand, if there is no strong set of associations in his mind clustered about the mood of depression, he may invent details which, on waking, seem inadequate to the mood. This fact accounts for the incommunicable wonder of a dream, as when at times we look back on the dream and are mystified at the seemingly unwarranted emotional responses which the details "aroused" in us. Trying to convey to others the emotional overtones of this dream, we laboriously recite the details, and are compelled at every turn to put in such confessions of defeat as "There was something strange about the room," or "For some reason or other I was afraid of this boat, although there doesn't seem to be any good reason now." But the details were not the cause of the emotion; the emotion, rather, dictated the selection of the details. Especially when the emotion was one of marvel or mystery, the invented details seem inadequate—the dream becoming, from the standpoint of communication, a flat failure, since the emotion failed to individuate itself into adequate symbols. And the sleeper himself, approaching his dream from the side of consciousness after the mood is gone, feels how inadequate are the details for conveying the emotion that caused them, and is aware that even for him the wonder of the dream exists only in so far as he still remembers the quality pervading it. Similarly, a dreamer may awaken himself with his own hilarious laughter, and be forthwith humbled as he recalls the witty saying of his dream. For the delight in the witty saying came first (was causally prior) and the witty saying itself was merely the externalization, or individuation, of this delight. Of a similar nature are the reminiscences of old men, who recite the facts of their childhood, not to force upon us the trivialities and minutiæ of these experiences, but in the forlorn hope of conveying to us the "overtones" of their childhood, overtones which, unfortunately, are beyond reach of the details which they see in such an incommunicable light, looking back as they do upon a past which is at once themselves and another.

The analogy between these instances and the procedure of the poet is apparent. In this way the poet's moods dictate the selection of details and thus individuate themselves into one specific work of art.

However, it may have been noticed that in discussing the crescendo and the dream I have been dealing with two different aspects of the art process. When art externalizes the human sense of crescendo by inventing one specific crescendo, this is much different from the dream externalizing depression by inventing a combination of details associated with depression. If the artist were to externalize his mood of horror by imagining the facts of a murder, he would still have to externalize his sense of crescendo by the arrangement of these facts. In the former case he is individuating an "emotional form," in the latter a "technical form." And if the emotion makes for the consistency of his details, by determining their selection, technique makes for the vigor, or saliency, or power of the art-work by determining its arrangement.[1]

---

[1] This saliency is, of course, best maintained by the shifting of technical forms. Any device for winning the attention, if too often repeated, soon becomes wearisome. Chesterton's constant conversion of his thoughts into paradox, for instance, finally inoculates us against the effect intended. Yet any one thought, given this form, is highly salient. The exploitation of a few technical forms produces *mannerism*, while the use of many produces *style*. A page of Shakespeare can be divided endlessly into technical devices (no doubt, for the most

COUNTER-STATEMENT

(Summary to this point)

We now have the poet with his moods to be individuated into subject-matter, and his feeling for technical forms to be individuated by the arrangement of this subject-matter. And as our poet is about to express himself, we must now examine the nature of self-expression.

First, we must recognize the element of self-expression which is in all activity. In both metaphysics and the sphere of human passions, the attraction of two objects has been called will, love, gravitation. Does water express itself when it seeks its level? Does the formation of a snow crystal satisfy some spiritual hunger awakened by the encroachment of chill upon dormant clouds? Foregoing these remoter implications, avoiding what need not here be solved, we may be content with recognizing the element of self-expression in all human activities. There is the expression of racial properties, types of self-expression common to all mankind, as the development from puberty to adolescence, the defense of oneself when in danger, the seeking of relaxation after labor. And there is the self-expression of personal characteristics: the development from puberty to adolescence mani-

part, spontaneously generated): shifting rhythms within the blank verse, coincidences and contrasts of vowel quantity, metaphors, epigrams, miniature plot processes where in a few lines some subject rises, blossoms, and drops—while above the whole is the march and curve of the central plot itself. Yet even Shakespeare tends to bludgeon us at times with the too frequent use of metaphor, until what was an allurement threatens to become an obstacle. We might say that the hypertrophy of metaphor is Shakespeare at his worst, and fills in those lapses of inspiration when he is keeping things going as best he can until the next flare-up. And thus, as with the music of Bach, if he at times attains the farthest reaches of luminosity and intensity, he never falls beneath the ingenious. . . . A writer like Proust, any single page of whom is astounding, becomes wearisome after extended reading. Proust's technical forms, one might say, are limited to the exploitation of parenthesis within parenthesis, a process which is carried down from whole chapters, through parts of chapters, into the paragraph, and thence into the halting of the single sentence.

festing itself in heightened religiosity, cruelty, sentimentality, or cynicism; the defense of oneself being procured by weapons, speech, law, or business; the relaxation after labor being sought in books rather than alcohol, alcohol rather than books, woman rather than either—or perhaps by a long walk in the country. One man attains self-expression by becoming a sailor, another by becoming a poet.

Self-expression today is too often confused with pure utterance, the spontaneous cry of distress, the almost reflex vociferation of triumph, the clucking of the pheasant as he is startled into flight. Yet such utterance is obviously but one small aspect of self-expression. And, if it is a form of self-expression to utter our emotions, it is just as truly a form of self-expression to provoke emotions in others, if we happen to prefer such a practice, even though the emotions aimed at were not the predominant emotions of our own lives. The maniac attains self-expression when he tells us that he is Napoleon; but Napoleon attained self-expression by commanding an army. And, transferring the analogy, the self-expression of the artist, *qua* artist, is not distinguished by the uttering of emotion, but by the evocation of emotion. If, as humans, we cry out that we are Napoleon, as artists we seek to command an army.

Mark Twain, before setting pen to paper, again and again transformed the bitterness that he *wanted* to utter into the humor that he *could* evoke. This would indicate that his desire to evoke was a powerful one; and an event which is taken by Mr. Van Wyck Brooks as an evidence of frustration can just as easily be looked upon as the struggle between two kinds of self-expression. We might say that Mark Twain, as artist, placed so much greater emphasis upon evocation than utterance that he would even change the burden of his message, evoking what he best could, rather than utter more and evoke less. Certain channels of expression will block others.

COUNTER-STATEMENT

To become an athlete, for instance, I must curb my appetite for food and drink; or I may glut and carouse, and regret to the end of my days the flabbiness of my muscles. Perhaps those critics, then, who would see us emancipated, who would show us a possible world of expression without frustration, mean simply that we are now free to go and storm a kingdom, to go and become Napoleons? In this they provide us with a philosophy of action rather than a method, and in the last analysis I fear that their theories are the self-expression of utterance, not a rigid system for compelling conviction, but a kind of standard for those of their own mind to rally about.

Thus, we will suppose that the artist, whom we have left for some time at the agonizing point of expressing himself, discovers himself not only with a message, but also with a desire to produce effects upon his audience. He will, if fortunate, attempt to evoke the feelings with which he himself is big; or else these feelings will undergo transformations (as in the case of Twain) before reaching their fruition in the art-work. Indeed, it is inevitable that all initial feelings undergo some transformation when being converted into the mechanism of art, and Mark Twain differs from less unhappy artists not in kind, but in degree. Art is a translation, and every translation is a compromise (although, be it noted, a compromise which may have new virtues of its own, virtues not part of the original). The mechanism invented to reproduce the original mood of the artist in turn develops independent requirements. A certain theme of itself calls up a counter-theme; a certain significant moment must be prepared for. The artist will add some new detail of execution because other details of his mechanism have created the need for it; hence while the originating emotion is still in ferment, the artist is concerned with impersonal mechanical processes. This leads to another set of considerations: *the artist's means are always tending to become ends in themselves.* The artist begins with his emotion, he translates this emotion into a mechanism for arousing emotion in others, and thus his interest in his own emotion transcends into his interest in the treatment. If we called beauty the artist's means of evoking emotion, we could say that the relationship between beauty and art is like that between logic and philosophy. For if logic is the implement of philosophy, it is just as truly the end of philosophy. The philosopher, as far as possible, erects his convictions into a logically progressive and well-ordered system of thought, because he would rather have such a system than one less well-ordered. So true is this, that at certain stages in the world's history when the content of philosophy has been thin, philosophers were even more meticulous than usual in their devotion to logical pastimes and their manipulation of logical processes. Which is to say that the philosopher does not merely use logic to convince others; he uses logic because he loves logic, so that logic is to him as much an end as a means. Others will aim at conviction by oratory, because they prefer rhetoric as a channel of expression. While in the Inquisition conviction was aimed at through the channel of physical torture, and presumably because the Inquisitors categorically enjoyed torture.[2] This consideration shows the poet as tending towards two extremes, or unilaterals: the extreme of utterance, which makes for the ideal of spontaneity and "pure" emotion, and leads to barbarism in art; and the extreme of pure beauty, or means conceived exclusively as end, which leads to virtu-

---

[2] Such a position, it has been contended, does not explain Demosthenes employing eloquence in his defense. We answer that it explains Demosthenes at a much earlier period when, with pebbles in his mouth, he struggled to perfect that medium which was subsequently to make his defense necessary. The medium which got him into trouble, he had to call upon to get him out of trouble.

osity, or decoration. And, in that fluctuating region between pure emotion and pure decoration, humanity and craftsmanship, utterance and performance, lies the field of art, the evocation of emotion by mechanism, a norm which, like all norms, is a conflict become fusion.

The poet steps forth, and his first step is the translation of his original mood into a symbol. So quickly has the mood become something else, no longer occupying the whole of the artist's attention, but serving rather as a mere indicator of direction, a principle of ferment. We may imagine the poet to suffer under a feeling of inferiority, to suffer sullenly and mutely until, being an artist, he spontaneously generates a symbol to externalize this suffering. He will write, say, of the King and the Peasant. This means simply that he has attained articulacy by linking his emotion to a technical form, and it is precisely this junction of emotion and technical form which we designate as the "germ of a plot," or "an idea for a poem." For such themes are merely the conversion of one's mood into a relationship, and the consistent observance of a relationship is the conscious or unconscious observance of a technical form. To illustrate:

In "The King and the Peasant" the technical form is one of contrast: the Humble and the Exalted. We might be shown the King and the Peasant, each in his sphere, each as a human being; but the "big scene" comes when the King is convoyed through the streets, and the Peasant bows speechless to the passing of the royal cortège. The Peasant, that is, despite all the intensity and subtlety of his personal experiences, becomes at this moment Peasant in the abstract—and the vestiture of sheer kingliness moves by . . . This basic relationship may be carried by variation into a new episode. The poet may arrange some incidents, the outcome of which is that the King and the Peasant find themselves in a common calamity, fleeing from some vast impersonal danger, a plague or an earthquake, which, like lightning, strikes regardless of prestige. Here King and Peasant are leveled as in death: both are Humble before the Exalted of unseen forces . . . The basic relationship may now be inverted. The King and the Peasant, say, are beset by brigands. There is a test of personal ingenuity or courage, it is the Peasant who saves the day, and lo! the Peasant is proved to be a true King and the King a Peasant.[3]

Our suppositional poet is now producing furiously, which prompts us to realize that his discovery of the symbol is no guaranty of good writing. If we may believe Jules Gaultier, Flaubert possessed genius in that he so ardently desired to be a genius; and we might say that this ratio was re-individuated into the symbol of Madame Bovary, a person trying to live beyond her station. This symbol in turn had to be carried down into a myriad details. But the symbol itself made for neither good writing nor bad. George Sand's symbols, which seemed equally adequate to encompass certain emotional and ideological complexities of her day, did not produce writing of such beauty. While as for Byron, we approach him less through the beauty of his workmanship than through our interest in, sympathy with, or aversion to, Byronism—Byronism being the quality behind such symbols as Manfred, Cain, and Childe Harold: the "man against the sky."

---

[3] This is, of course, an overly simplified example of technical form as a generative principle, yet one can cite the identical procedure in a noble poem, *Lycidas*. After repeating for so long in varying details the idea that Lycidas is dead while others are left behind to mourn him ("But, oh! the heavy change, now thou art gone . . .") Milton suddenly reverses the ratio:

> "Weep no more, woeful shepherds, weep no more,
> For Lycidas, your sorrow, is not dead."

Lycidas lives on in Heaven. Which is to say, it is Lycidas, and not his mourners, who is truly alive!

This brings up the matter of relationship between the symbol and the beautiful.

This symbol, I should say, attracts us by its power of formula, exactly as a theory of history or science. If we are enmeshed in some nodus of events and the nodus of emotions surrounding those events, and someone meets us with a diagnosis (simplification) of our partially conscious, partially unconscious situation, we are charmed by the sudden illumination which this formula throws upon our own lives. Mute Byrons (potential Byrons) were waiting in more or less avowed discomfiture for the formulation of Byronism, and when it came they were enchanted. Again and again through Byron's pages they came upon the minutiæ of their Byronism (the ramifications of the symbol) and continued enchanted. And thus, the symbol being so effective, they called the work of Byron beautiful. By which they meant that it was successful in winning their emotions.

But suppose that I am not Byronic, or rather that the Byronic element in me is subordinated to other much stronger leanings. In proportion as this is so, I shall approach Byron, not through his Byronism, but through his workmanship (not by the ramifications of the symbol, but by the manner in which these ramifications are presented). Byronism will not lead me to accept the workmanship; I may be led, rather, by the workmanship to accept Byronism. Calling only those parts of Byron beautiful which lead me to accept Byronism, I shall find less of such beauty than will all readers who are potential Byrons. Here technical elements mark the angle of my approach, and it will be the technical, rather than the symbolic, elements of the poet's mechanism that I shall find effective in evoking my emotions, and thus it will be in these that I shall find beauty. For beauty is the term we apply to the poet's success in evoking our emotions.

Falstaff may, I think, be cited as an almost perfect symbol

from the standpoint of approach through workmanship, for nearly all readers are led to Falstaff solely through the brilliancy of his presentation. The prince's first speech, immediately before Falstaff himself has entered, strikes a theme and a pace which startles us into attention. Thereafter, again and again the enormous obligations which the poet has set himself are met with, until the character of this boisterous "bedpresser" becomes for us one of the keenest experiences in all literature. If one needs in himself the itch of Byronism to meet Byron halfway, for the enjoyment of Falstaff he needs purely the sense of literary values.

Given the hour, Flaubert must share the honors with George Sand. But when the emphasis of society has changed, new symbols are demanded to formulate new complexities, and the symbols of the past become less appealing of themselves. At such a time Flaubert, through his greater reliance upon style, becomes more "beautiful" than Sand. Although I say this realizing that historical judgments are not settled once and for all, and some future turn of events may result in Sand's symbols again being very close to our immediate concerns, while Flaubert might by the same accident become remote: and at such a time Flaubert's reputation would suffer. In the case of his more romantic works, this has already happened. In these works we feel the failures of workmanship, especially his neglect of an organic advancement or progression, a neglect which permits only our eye to move on from page to page while our emotions remain static, the lack of inner co-ordination making it impossible for us to accumulate momentum in a kind of work which strongly demands such momentum, such "anticipation and remembering." This becomes for us an insurmountable obstacle, since the symbols have ceased to be the "scandals" they were for his contemporaries, so that we demand technique where they inclined more to content themselves with "message." And thus only too often we find the *Temptations of Saint Anthony* not beautiful, but decorative, less an experience than a performance.

Yet we must not consider the symbol, in opposition to style, as outside of technical form. The technical appeal of the symbol lies in the fact that it is a principle of logical guidance, and makes for the repetition of itself in changing details which preserve as a constant the original ratio. A study of evolution, for instance, may be said to repeat again and again, under new aspects, the original proposition of evolution. And in the same way the symbol of art demands a continual restatement of itself in all the ramifications possible to the artist's imagination.[4]

---

[4] It is usually in works of fantasy that this repetition of the symbol under varying aspects can be followed most easily. In *Gulliver's Travels,* for instance, the ratio of discrepancy between Gulliver and his environment is repeated again and again in new subject-matter. The ratio of the *Odyssey* is ramified in a manner which is equally obvious, being, we might say, the discovery of the propositions which were, for Homer, inherent in the idea of "man in the wide, wide world." In its purity, this repetition of the symbol's ratio usually makes for episodic plot, since precisely this repetition is the *primum mobile* of the story. Baudelaire's sonnet, *La Géante,* is a perfect instance of the episodic in miniature. Thus, in the more exuberant days, when nature created monsters, the poet would have liked to live with a giantess, like a cat with a queen; he would have peered into the fogs of her eyes; he would have crawled over the slope of her enormous knees; and when, tired, she stretched out across the countryside, he would have "slept nonchalantly beneath the shadows of her breasts, like a peaceful hamlet at the foot of a mountain." . . . This same deduction is, of course, at the bottom of every successful art-work, although where accumulation is more in evidence than linear progression (incidents of plot being "brought to a head") these simple ratios are more deeply embedded, and thus less obvious. In his monologues, his conversations with the ghost, with Polonius, with Ophelia, with his mother—in each of these instances Hamlet repeats, under a new aspect, the same "generative ratio," that symbol and enigma which is Hamlet. "A certain kind of person" is a static symbol; a murder is a dynamic one; but beneath the dynamic we will find the static.

In closing: We have the original emotion, which is channelized into a symbol. This symbol becomes a generative force, a relationship to be repeated in varying details, and thus makes for one aspect of technical form. From a few speeches of Falstaff, for instance, we advance unconsciously to a synthesis of Falstaff; and thereafter, each time he appears on the stage, we know what to expect of him in essence, or quality, and we enjoy the poet's translation of this essence, or quality, into particulars, or quantity. The originating emotion makes for *emotional* consistency within the parts; the symbol demands a *logical* consistency within this emotional consistency. In a horror story about a murder, for instance, the emotion of horror will suggest details associated with horror, but the specific symbol of murder will limit the details of horror to those adapted to murder.[5]

The symbol faces two ways, for in addition to the technical form just mentioned (an "artistic" value) it also applies to life, serving here as a formula for our experiences, charming us by finding some more or less simple principle underlying our emotional complexities. For the symbol here affects us like a work of science, like the magic formula of the savage, like the medicine for an ill. But the symbol is also like a "message," in that once we know it we feel no call to return to it, except in our memories, unless some new element of appeal is to be found there. If we read again and again some textbook on evolution, and enjoy quoting aloud pages of it, this is because, beyond the message, there is style. For in addition to the symbol, and the ramifications of the

[5] Some modern writers have attempted, without great success, to eliminate the symbol, and thus to summon the *emotional* cluster without the further limitation of a *logical* unity. This is also true of modern music. Compare, for instance, the constant circulation about a theme in classical music with the modern disregard of this "arbitrary" unity. As story today gravitates towards lyric, so sonata gravitates towards suite.

symbol, poetry also involves the *method of presenting* these ramifications. We have already shown how a person who does not avidly need the symbol can be led to it through the excellence of its presentation. And we should further realize that the person who does avidly need the symbol loses this need the more thoroughly the symbol is put before him. I may be startled at finding myself Faust or Hamlet, and even be profoundly influenced by this formulation, since something has been told me that I did not know before. But I cannot repeat this new and sudden "illumination." Just as every religious experience becomes ritualized (artistic values taking the place of revelation) so when I return to the symbol, no matter how all-sufficient it was at the first, the test of repetition brings up a new factor, which is style.

"What we find words for," says Nietzsche, "is that for which we no longer have use in our own hearts. There is always a kind of contempt in the act of speaking." Contempt, indeed, so far as the original emotion was concerned, but not contempt for the act of speaking.

THE STATUS OF ART

IN THE nineteenth century, when much was brought into question, many things previously called good had to be defended — poetry among them. Wherefore the slogan of *Art for Art's Sake* which, though it was often pronounced with bravado, clearly had about it the element of a "justification." With the development of technology, "usefulness" was coming into prominence as a test of values, so that art's slogan was necessarily phrased to take the criterion of usefulness into account. The strategy of the artist is understandable enough. Against the accusation that art was "useless," he pitted the challenge that art was important to those to whom art was important. Nevertheless, his position could readily take on the appearance of a "last stand."

The original doctrines of art's "uselessness" were not offered as attacks upon art. Kant, in proposing "purposiveness without purpose" (*Zweckmässigkeit ohne Zweck*) as a formula for the æsthetic, had no intention of providing a "refutation" of art. His formula did, however, mark the emergence of the "use" criterion which was subsequently to place all purely intellectual pursuits upon a defensive basis. His proposition could be readily perverted: if the æsthetic had no *purpose* outside itself, the corollary seemed to be that the æsthetic had no *result* outside itself. Logically there was no cogency in such an argument, but psychologically there was a great deal. And the damage was perhaps increased through attempts to justify art by the postulating of a special "art instinct" or "æsthetic sense."

On the face of it, this was a good move. For at a time when instincts were gaining considerably in repute, and no complicated human mind could arouse us to admiration so

63

promptly as the routine acts of an insect, what could be more salubrious for the reputation of art than the contention that art satisfies an "instinctive need"? The trouble arose from the fact that the "art instinct" was associated with the "play instinct," thus becoming little more than an adult survival from childhood. The apologists, still in the Kantian scheme, associated art with play because both seemed, from the standpoint of utility, purposeless. But in an age when "work" was becoming one of society's basic catchwords, art could not very well be associated with play without some loss of prestige.

Perhaps Flaubert's constant talk of toil was prompted in part by a grudging awareness of the new criterion. At least, his complaints serve to make this form of "play" a colossal task. Remy de Gourmont saw the issue clearly enough to use a complete reversal of standards in his defense of art, ridiculing the "serious" as a democratic preference, and insisting that the things of essential human value were gratuitous, hardly more than unforeseen mutations, qualities obtained *in spite of* society, and worthy of cultivation even though they might be found, not merely useless, but positively subversive to social ends. The position was vigorously taken—and doubtless De Gourmont's able championship of the symbolists had much to do with the advancing of their experiments. De Gourmont was bright; he was very handy with ideas; he could carry the discussion aggressively into the territory of the enemy. He made one think of literature as a risk, a kind of outlawry, with the notable exception that the outlaws were in reality the true preservers of the good. Art would eventually be driven into the catacombs, he said, thus associating the artist with both rebellion and virtue at once. It was not until shortly before the war, however, that De Gourmont became an "authority"—and his influence collapsed soon afterwards as he was prevented by death from bolstering it up with new books. For many of the critical and philosophical matters he treated had since been handled in other terms and with more thoroughness by other men— and his fiction, necessarily restricted by his cloistered existence, could not bear the diffusion of his great productivity and his attempted breadth. Furthermore, ironic detachment is a difficult position to uphold when men are being copiously slaughtered—and De Gourmont's enlistment in the cause of the Allies implied the renunciation of his earlier doctrines. Disciples of Art for Art's Sake might advocate art as a refuge, a solace for the grimness about them, but the spirit of social mockery could no longer fit the scene. One can mock death, but one cannot mock men in danger of death. In the presence of so much disaster, there was no incentive to call art disastrous.

But if De Gourmont had seen the issues clearly enough to realize that one might best defend art by calling art "immoral," most critics attempted the compromise of defending art as "amoral" or "unmoral." Their invented adjective probably did wonders to assist the introduction of new social values and to procure, for many an artist's ethical innovations, asylum from the law. The word was needed, as the artist's position was a particularly difficult one. The scientists of the nineteenth century, despite the thoroughness of their attacks upon traditional values, could be very circumspect in their methods. Though the tenets of anthropology, for instance, might imply the discrediting of orthodox religion, one could discuss them adequately without handling the matter in this light at all. Art, on the other hand, must be first of all "forceful." The artist, in dealing with ethical revaluations (as he naturally would, since the characteristics of the century would be as fully represented in him as in a scientist or an inventor) had to make those conflicts explicit which the scientist could leave implicit. He got his effects by throwing into relief those very issues which the scientist could treat by circumlocution, implication, and the mystical protection of a technical vocabulary. Thus, whereas science for the most part was permitted to progress in peace, the artistic equivalents of this science produced a succession of scandals.

An incident in Flaubert's trial indicates the nature of the artist's predicament. The prosecuting attorney selected among others a passage from *Madame Bovary* which described Emma undressing in the presence of her lover. The rhythm of this passage very obviously contributed to the effect, since it suggested her impatience as she struggled with her garments, and her final impetuosity as she rushed across the room to embrace him. The prosecuting attorney read this passage with feeling—and the better he read it, the worse the case for Flaubert. The defense lawyer, however, sought to remove the impression by reading the same passage himself and interpolating remarks of his own which ruined the passage as literature. The more ineffective he made it, the more pardonable Flaubert became!

The term "unmoral" was a valuable discovery for handling the situation. By this subterfuge (surely no one thought of it as such) the artist could plead immunity from judgment by any code of practical ethics. In keeping with the doctrine of the "unmorality" of art, we must distinguish between virtuous conduct and virtuous sentences, we must not restrict art as we should restrict its equivalent in actual life, we must not limit the laws of the "beautiful" by the laws of social behavior. But "unmorality" was in the end a much greater danger to the prestige of art than "immorality" could ever have been, since it implied once again the ineffectiveness of art.

As a matter of fact, art exerted a tremendous influence upon the changing morals and customs of the Western world, but its contribution to the "transvaluation of values" was minimized because of this apologetic adjective. Art was, as De Gourmont said, "immoral." It was, that is, using its expressiveness as a means of making people seek what they customarily fled and flee what they customarily sought. And there is no greater evidence of art's "immorality" than the bourgeois–Bohemian conflict which characterized the century. The issue was indeterminate and fluctuant, but in the main the disciples of Art for Art's Sake were Bohemians, prepared on many occasions to outrage the bourgeois.

In some respects they were struggling to alter the moral code in keeping with the changes brought about by science and technology (a tendency which, in its purely artistic manifestations, is to be seen in the extending of the "beautiful" into the realm of the previously repugnant). In this they were really working for the bourgeois interests, though the bourgeois public was prompt to resist them. In other respects, however, they were not *devanciers* at all but were, like such men as T. S. Eliot today, the preservers of older standards which the bourgeois themselves were attempting to discredit. Baudelaire was attacked as a destroyer of the earlier moral code, but as a matter of fact he was opposing the new social code. Baudelaire is a "sinner," and what is more alien to the new social code than the concept of sin? Baudelaire courts poverty, lamentation, sullenness, a discipline of internal strife; his concerns are the concerns of an early Christian anchorite voluntarily placing himself in jeopardy—and what could be more "conservative" than this, what more unlike the young Californian with his benign circle of culture, progress, and prosperity, or his football conception of discipline? In most instances the division was not so intense, the artists being the defenders simply of older humanistic doctrines overlooked in the rising intensity of economic strife. In general they tended towards Pater's belief that ethics should be a subdivision of æsthetics. The artists were innovators and conservators at once, advocating many requisite alterations of morality while attempting to preserve many cultural values of the past which seemed equally requisite. Thus can such an innovator as Eliot be found saying: "We fight rather to keep something alive than in the expectation that anything will triumph."

In general, therefore, a division between artist and bourgeois was emphasized. And here again the alignment was greatly to the detriment of art, as many trivial artists, and even some artists of rank, chose to exploit this division by making their opposition more picturesque than ominous. Hence arose the "æsthete," whose adherence to the doctrine of Art for Art's Sake served to associate the doctrine with many effete mannerisms. Wilde is perhaps the purest symbol of the type — and Wilde is as responsible as anyone for the weakening of the bourgeois–Bohemian conflict. The next generation of authors married at twenty, courted the strictest conventionality of dress and manners, and tended to consider a few years in business as the new educational equivalent of the European tour.

The bourgeois–Bohemian conflict had another unfavorable feature in its alliance with the rise of symbolism. Symbolism contained one important alteration in method. In emphasizing the emotional connection of ideas and images, it tended to suppress their commoner experimental or "logical" connections. Instead of saying that something was like something else, the symbolist progressed from the one thing to the other by ellipsis. He would not tell us that a toothache is a raging storm—rather, he might advance directly from the mention of a diseased tooth to the account of a foundering ship. Objects are thus linked by their less obvious connectives. This is, of course, an over-simplification of symbolist methods, but it is roughly indicative. Whether it is correct or not, however, the fact remains that while the artist was attempting new departures in methodology, he was not matching his imaginative experiments with their equivalents in critical theory. To an extent he was probably uncertain as to the exact critical principles underlying the new tendencies. And taking his cue from the earlier moral conflict between bourgeois and Bohemian, he now widened the conflict to include questions of method. Far from pleading with his public, the artist heightened his antagonism: hence his readiness to *épater le bourgeois*. Art now took on a distinctly obscurantist trait, not because it was any more "obscure" than previous art (nothing is more obscure than an after-dinner speaker's distinctions between optimism and over-optimism, yet no one is troubled by them) but because the public had not been schooled as to just wherein the clarity of such art was to be sought. The vagueness of the issue made a good deal of slovenly work possible — and even men in sympathy with the movement had to confess themselves "defeated" by many of its proponents.

Closely allied with the "mystification" of the new movement, came the *tour d'ivoire* or "pure" art movement. The most pretentious writing, that is, was done by men whose methods and preoccupations seemed certain to limit their reading public considerably. They were "experts," and nothing was more abhorrent to a civilization of specialists than artists who likewise were specialists. (It seems that, beginning with the pre-historic bard, the artist had always been a specialist, but people never resented the fact until, by becoming specialists themselves, they became less fit to follow him.) In any event, the rarity and electness of "pure" art seemed—in an age of propaganda—negative, retiring, and powerless. What was the value of neglected excellence, when the world was glutted with crude fiction? Had not the spread of literacy through compulsory education made readers of people who had no genuine interest in literature? Would not this group henceforth form the majority of the reading public? And would not good books pale into insignificance, not because they had fewer readers than in the past (they had more) but because an overwhelming army of bad readers had been recruited? The Art for Art's Sake slogan now began to apply more specifically to the art of the minority, those writers for whom, so far as the vast public was concerned, the publication of a new work was like putting a bottle out to sea.

A masterpiece, privately printed in a limited edition of two hundred copies, seemed to furnish some cause for derision. Yet *The Little Review* had a much larger circulation than the magazine published by Goethe and Schiller. And one must recall that most of the works fed to the public are purely derivative, and as such can constitute the bridge between the "rare" writer and the public at large. The same basic patterns of thought can be exemplified either in subtle ways or in a crude form for the consumption of millions. Through such derivative processes, for instance, the public of today is undergoing the influence of nineteenth century writers whom, for one reason or another, it would not at all care to read. It is coming to accept methods which, but a few years ago, were confined to the most "abstruse." In general the "rare" writers will serve as "sources," for only a man whose attitudes arise from the persistency of his character can be expected to work with them until they have acquired a forbidding distinction and to express them with such thoroughness and penetration as makes his work unacceptable to the majority. The vulgarizers, however, the epigons, the "steppers-down" will adapt this source material for wider reception. Indeed, when we consider how few masters of theology there were in the early Church, how small was their reading public, yet how great was their influence upon the course of history, we realize that a work can, by devious ways, profoundly affect people who have never laid eyes upon it. A single book, were it greatly to influence one man in a position of authority, could thus indirectly alter the course of a nation; and similarly the group that turns to "minority" art may be a "pivotal" group. They need not be "pivotal" in the sense that they enjoy particular social, political, or economic prestige—but purely in the sense that they are more articulate and enterprising in the assertion of their views and the communication of their attitudes. Nor must we, recalling Eliot's statement, assume that one cannot be an influence except by "succeeding." The rôle of opposition is by no means negligible in the shaping of society. The victory of one "principle" in history is usually not the vanquishing, but the partial incorporation, of another.

As for the concerns of a "neglected minority," it is hard to understand how any cultural movement could begin otherwise than in a very restricted quarter, spreading by radiation from the few who are quickest to sense new factors in their incipient stages. Astute politicians, it is true, will tell us that a political movement must arise "from the grass roots." It must, they say, spring up spontaneously in various parts of the country, a party serving merely to consolidate it into a united front. But the artist exploits human potentialities in a different way than a politician. If thirty million people are eager for a trip to the country, a book might gain great popularity through enabling them to imagine that they were in the country. Yet not one of them would have to know that their weariness with city living was the cause of the book's appeal. The politician, on the other hand, could not safely back a new bond issue for the suburbanizing of his city until his constituents' preferences were clearly and vocally established. A politician seeks to ally himself, actually or apparently, with issues which to his mind the people consciously advocate. An artist can appeal tremendously by the utilization of motives which both he and they are unaware of. It is obvious that a situation must be widespread before a method for handling it can find general reception. But it is the *situation,* not the *method,* that rises "from the grass roots." Let the situation be tinder, and the method may "catch like wildfire"; but the spark is not integral to the situation, it must be added. The "times were ripe" for a Byron; but Byronism radiated from an individual. A slogan is not widely effective because it rises spontaneously in every part of the country (it is usually one man's invention); a slogan is widely effective because it is appropriate to a widespread situation. And thus a work of art may at times be confined to a minority, not because of either its virtues or its defects, but purely because the particular situation with which it is dealing is not generally felt. Indeed, by the time the situation has become generally felt, this particular work of art may still be inappropriate for another reason: it may happen to have dealt with the situation in conventions which have since altered. And thus it will serve, not in itself, but in the suggestions it gave to a writer of the day who "translates" them into his contemporary conventions.

II

Perhaps none of the issues so far discussed had so adverse an effect upon the status of art as certain "causation" theories which seemed to place art as a kind of by-product, the result of more vital and important forces. Doctrines of psychology, economics, and world history have all been used with nearly evangelical zeal to undermine the sanctions of the "impractical." Thus, the psychoanalyst's analogies between art and dream-life, while not formulated as an attack upon art, readily came to serve as one. For how could we transfer to art

the dream relationship between frustration and wish-fulfill-
ment without seeming to indicate a fundamental ineffectualness on the part of the artist? The doctrine could be manipu-
lated to reveal the artist purely as a "thwarted" individual
who was compensating for his inabilities by dreaming of
triumphs.

In noting the similarity between art and dream-life, the
psychoanalytic critics failed to note the important dissimi-
larity, an oversight somewhat justified by the fact that the
theorists of individualism in art had themselves made the
same omission. They did not consider that, whereas a dream
is wholly subjective, all competent art is a means of communication, however vague the artist's conception of his
audience may be. Thus, the analogies summarily dismissed
the important qualification that day-dreaming generally
makes exceptionally bad art. The many aspects of analysis,
discovery, observation, diction, revision, tactics in presentation, which are anything but "day-dreaming," were wholly
ignored. And in their eagerness to point out the artist's maladjustments, the psychoanalytic critics did not take into
account the elements of strength often implicated in such
maladjustments. Maladjustments were too readily assumed
to be evidences of weakness. But there is much in Nietzsche,
for instance, to indicate that his maladjustments arose from
his searching perception of issues which were wholly un-
noted by his more "fit" contemporaries. Is it a sign of "weakness" to see with such intensity that one can disclose "conflicts" and encounter "defeats" where hackmen find nothing?

Again, few considered the fact that, by psychoanalytic
tenets, practical activities as well as imaginative ones can constitute "compensations" for frustrated conditions. To every
poet who became a poet after failure in business, there are
at least a hundred business men who became business men
after failure in poetry. And psychoanalysis had given many

instances of deflection and frustration in practical life. Nothing was more prevalent in its case histories than examples of intense practical activities stimulated by the pressure of an unsuccessful love affair or some unavowed desire. A cruel impulse can be "sublimated" into a philanthropic act as well as into a philanthropic poem. Napoleons themselves were credited with such "inferiority complexes" as were supposed to motivate the artist.[1]

And if the artist turns to art rather than to business or baseball, his choice need not have anything negative about it. Eliminate the medical terminology and you eliminate the disease. The great amount of annoyance which an artist generally undergoes to establish himself in his craft would indicate a very positive preference for this craft. Far from being "in retreat," he must master ways of exerting influence upon the minds and emotions of others. Could anything be less like regression, though one were to write on a desert island? True, one cannot devote himself greatly to a single pursuit without endangering his competence in others, though the predicament applies as much to engineering or farming as to art. An artist such as Beethoven, whose musical

[1] Until psychoanalysis defines a social norm, we are logically at liberty to interpret any activity (either contemplative or practical) as an "avoidance" of some other contemplative or practical activity. A man chopping down trees can be said to avenge himself against the entanglements of an emotion by this vicarious cutting of Gordian knots; or we can look upon Rimbaud's flight into Africa as a practical means of avoiding the æsthetic dilemma into which he had placed himself. Let us further note the "heads I win, tails you lose" mechanism which the psychoanalysts have at their disposal. Having defined the nature of a man's psychosis, they can fit any act into the scheme. For if the act follows the same pattern as the psychosis, they can explain it as consistent—but if it does not follow this pattern, they can account for it as "sublimated" or "compensatory." With such *vaticinium post eventum* (such explanation by epicycles) at their command, there is no reason why they should ever be at a loss for explanations in keeping with their tenets.

attainments seemed to require great specialization and concentration, would necessarily become a bungler in other aspects of social intercourse. The intensity of his character gave him greater turmoil than most men must learn to subdue by the compromises and tactics of social advantage, while the many hours devoted to music left him much less opportunity than most men require to perfect themselves in social matters. Thus his specialization in music could lead to his inadequacy in other things, and his inadequacy in other things could give him further incentive to specialize in that pursuit wherein he was a master — the interactions are too confusing for anyone to dare call the inadequacies exclusively a "cause" and the art exclusively an "effect." A man may become æsthetically entangled because of some sexual difficulty — but he may as truly become sexually entangled because of some æsthetic difficulty; and many a prowler would gladly sacrifice his night if he could but write a good paragraph by doing so.

Art must have a subject, and a spontaneous subject. And what could be a more spontaneous subject for the artist than the matter of his maladjustments? Is not every man concerned primarily with his "problems"? Is the case different with the scientist, the explorer, the business man? Is not genius, in whatever channel it appears, distinguished by the persistence of its preoccupations — and are not man's preoccupations essentially a matter of volition, and hence of frustration? And that a man, let us say incestuously troubled, should express this trouble in his art, is no more an indication of weakness than that a man raised in Australia should paint Australian landscapes.

And as for the "escape" of art, there is much to indicate that the artist is, of all men, equipped to confront an issue. The very conventions of art often provide him with a method for freely admitting experiences and situations which the practical man must conceal. And psychologists of other schools have noted that whereas intensity of fear or pain will generally produce in most people a kind of "stereotypy," a mental and physical numbing which leaves the individual almost without memory of the painful or terrifying event, great artists have shown capacity to keep themselves receptive at precisely such moments. They may bear the full brunt of an experience without psychological evasions, because their attitude enables them to feel partially as opportunity what others must feel solely as a menace. This ability does not, I believe, derive from exceptional strength; it probably arises purely from the "professional interest" the artist may take in his difficulties; and I cite the distinction, not as evidence of unusual power on the artist's part, but simply as evidence that the need of "escape" by subterfuge is more natural to the man whose problems are exclusively practical than to the man whose outlook upon his difficulties is partially æsthetic.[2]

Ironically enough, the point on which the psychoanalytic critics paid the highest tribute to art turned out to be perhaps the strongest attack of all. I refer to the great emphasis upon intensity of experience which such criticism associated with the work of art. There is no reason why the enjoyment of a work of art should not be intense, to be sure; the danger arose from the fact that actual and imaginative experiences were not distinguished. Now, once one is taught to seek in

[2] Under extremely distasteful conditions one builds a wall of anæsthesia and forgetfulness, contrives mental ways of leaving pain unregistered. Yet a man may, in undergoing stress, meet it without safeguards of this sort. He may accept its full impact, may let it pour down upon him, as though he were putting his face up into a thundershower. If he survives, the period of stress is not a period of blankness, but a period of great intricacy and subtlety which lives on in the memory and can be drawn upon. The artist's technique of articulation often enables him to admit what other men, by emotional subterfuges, deny.

art such experiences as one gets in life itself, it is a foregone conclusion that one must discover how trivial are artistic experiences as compared with "real living." A mere headache is more "authentic" than a great tragedy; the most dismal love affair is more worth experiencing in actual life than the noblest one in a poem. When the appeal of art as method is eliminated and the appeal of art as experience is stressed, art seems futile indeed. Experience is less the *aim* of art than the *subject* of art; art is not *experience,* but *something added* to experience. But by making art and experience synonymous, a critic provides an unanswerable reason why a man of spirit should renounce art forever.

The economic attack upon art arose in an equally roundabout and unintended manner. It involved essentially a theory of meaning, though it might have become more defensible dialectically had it been developed with a clearer understanding of its basis. Noting that certain great works of the past were "imperiled" by subsequent changes of history, critics influenced by the tenets of evolutionism held that to appreciate a work we must understand the environmental conditions out of which it arose. The Greek tragedies are now unsatisfactory to most of us, the "genetic" critic argued, because we are too unfamiliar with the structure of Greek society implicated in these tragedies. To "restore" the full value of these tragedies, we must steep ourselves in their social context.

The point is irrefutable. Insofar as a social context changes, the work of art erected upon it is likely to change in evaluation (though the genetic critic does not tell us whether we should also apply his method to an artist whose reputation has risen with the years—whether we should, by placing Melville in his times, "restore" to him the inferior position he held among his contemporaries). If Swift, in *Gulliver's*

Travels, makes a sly gibe at some current political intrigue now forgotten, the modern reader must have the relevant environmental facts of this intrigue restored for him by editorial annotation before he can appreciate the full "meaning" of Swift's sentence. It may also have "meaning" as fancy, which is its meaning for a child, or for a reader lacking the editorial annotation, or for one of Swift's contemporaries unaware of the political intrigue Swift had in mind; but for its full meaning as Swift meant it, we must perceive its equivocal nature. An element of Swift's social context was here involved in his meaning, the words themselves not being an adequate statement of the situation. Similarly a knowledge of Plato's archetypes may be useful in reading of Wordsworth's clouds of glory; the *Divine Comedy* uses aspects of scholastic thinking which are no longer current and the recovery of which is essential; when we read, "Speak to it, Horatio, you are a scholar," we must know, or be able to infer, that erudition was once supposed to enable its possessor to talk with ghosts.

In some cases the matter to be recovered is so remote, is in a channel of thinking or feeling so alien to our own, that even a savant's "restoration" of the environmental context is not adequate. This is always true in some degree — though historical relativists have tended to make too much of it. For in the last analysis, any reader surrounds each word and each act in a work of art with a *unique* set of his own previous experiences (and therefore a unique set of imponderable emotional reactions), communication existing in the "margin of overlap" between the writer's experience and the reader's. And while it is dialectically true that two people of totally different experiences must totally fail to communicate, it is also true that there are no two such people, the "margin of overlap" always being considerable (due, if to nothing else, to the fact that man's biologic functions are uniform). Absolute communication between ages is impossible in the same way that absolute communication between contemporaries is impossible. And conversely, as we communicate approximately though "imprisoned within the walls of our personality," so we communicate approximately though imprisoned within the walls of our age.

The historical approach may have affected the status of art slightly by questioning art's "permanence" (a roadbed was not expected to meet the same rigorous requirement). But the "practicality" shibboleth, as introduced by the economic critic, converted this genetic theory of social contexts into a causation theory, with economic forces as prime movers and art as a mere "result." If art arises out of a social context, the economic critic argued, art is "caused" by the social context. And thence, by simplifying the concept of social context to exclude all but political and economic factors, he could interpret art as the mere reflection of contemporary political and economic issues.

To begin with, the theories of meaning that underlie the historical or environmental approach could not properly be converted into a system of causation. If I say that "white" has certain connotations because snow is white, I certainly am not saying that a work of art using these connotations is "caused" by snow. I am simply saying that the meaning of white to an Eskimo will differ from its meaning to a mid-African, and that a work of art constructed about the mid-African's connotations of "white" may be inappropriate to a reader who approaches it with the "white" experiences of an Eskimo. Or if people hold a certain doctrine, a work of art can exploit their belief to make them, let us say, feel terror; if they hold the opposite doctrine, the work of art can similarly exploit this opposite belief to make them feel terror. The work that arouses terror by exploiting the one belief will be imperiled at the hands of any reader who holds to the opposite belief; but could we say that either work is "caused" by the belief which it exploits?

Reduced to its essentials, the encroachment of a causation doctrine here seems to be statable as follows: Changes in art occur concomitantly with changes in political and economic conditions; therefore the changes in art are caused by the changes in political and economic conditions. At times the process is removed one step further, the changes in art being attributed in turn to changes in economic conditions. Now, it is not very sound dialectic to assume that, because two things change concomitantly, one can be called exclusively a cause of the other. If mere concurrence can prove causation, why could not an opponent assume from the same facts that the changes in art and ideas caused the changes in economic conditions? We know, for example, that the feminist "æsthetic" served as preparation for the enfranchisement of women: here is an obvious example of an attitude's affecting a change in social structure.

In one sense, art or ideas do "reflect" a situation, since they are a way of dealing with a situation. When a man solves a problem, however, we should hardly say that his solution is "caused" by the problem to be solved. The problem may limit somewhat the *nature* of his solution, but the problem can remain unsolved forever unless he *adds* the solution. Similarly, the particular ways of feeling and seeing which the thinker or the artist develop to cope with a situation, the vocabulary they bring into prominence, the special kinds of intellectual and emotional adjustment which their works make possible by the discovery of appropriate symbols for encompassing the situation, the kinds of action they stimulate by their attitudes towards the situation, are not "caused" by the situation which they are designed to handle. The theory of economic causation seemed to rest upon the assumption that there is only one possible æsthetic response to a given situation, and that this situation is solely an economic one.

Our argument is not intended as a plea for free will. It may be true that, if we knew every single factor involved in a stimulus, we could infallibly predict the response. It may be true that, despite our "illusion of liberty," we are rigidly determined in both our thoughts and our actions. Even if we grant the validity of this principle, however, the doctrine of the economic determination of art need not be conceded. For by any principle of universal determinism, there would be no hierarchy of causes whereby economic manifestations could be called causally "prior" to æsthetic manifestations. Economic and æsthetic manifestations alike would be caused by the "nature of things." If determinism is extended to such cosmic proportions, art need have no complaint. For by the tenets of determinism as so extended, every factor of experience would be equally involved in the causal chain, being indeterminately cause and effect, the effect of one event and the cause of another. And in a scheme whereby we "all go down together," the appropriateness of art has long ago been established, as in the ethical teachings of the Roman Stoics. Drive the logic of economic causation to the point where economic determinism becomes cosmic determinism, and the detractors of art are necessarily silenced, for their own detractions become but the output of the universal mill, their preferences mere personal choices devoid of "absolute" sanction.

Yet recent years have witnessed an attempt to manipulate precisely this argument of cosmic determination in such a way that the pursuit of art can be discredited and the criterion of "use" once more put forward. I refer to Oswald Spengler's "morphology of history." While accepting the logical conclusion of cosmic determinism so far as the attempt at a hierarchy of causes is concerned, and thus placing economic and æsthetic manifestations on a par, he proposes nonetheless to

81

See preface, xiv for more on Spengler.

draw forth an exhortation for the abandonment of art as ineffectual. The evidence by which he supports his thesis has been brought into question, but that need not concern us here, as we are examining primarily the dialectic of his proof. We are discussing the logical issue as to whether the thesis, even if established, would justify his exhortation to abandon art. The steps of his argument are worth following in detail, as his work is the most ambitious schematization of its sort, and its dilemma is typical of the dilemma confronting all such programs.

Over against the H. G. Wells concept of history as a straight line progressing from savagery to modernity, Spengler opposes the concept of numberless cultural systems, each of which has followed a cycle of its own, growing, flourishing, and decaying in a fixed order or "periodicity." These cultural cycles, by Spengler's doctrine, evolve in an irreversible sequence through "spring, summer, autumn, and winter" aspects, any "season" of one culture being comparable with the corresponding season of any other culture. These analogous stages of different cultural systems are called "contemporaneous"; and by aligning the stages of our own cultural cycle (that of Europe and European America, which Spengler dates from about 1000 A.D.) with the contemporaneous stages of other cultural cycles, Spengler claims to produce a series of co-ordinates for determining which of the cultural seasons is now upon us.

Homer, in the Græco-Roman cycle, would be contemporaneous with the northern sagas in our own, this era always being "rural and intuitive," and marked by the "birth of a myth in the grand style, expressing a new sense of divinity." Spring gradually metamorphoses into summer, a period of "ripening consciousness" and of the "earliest urban and critical stirrings"—the pre-Socratics of the sixth and fifth centuries being "contemporaneous" with Galileo, Bacon, and

Descartes. In autumn the city assumes a leading position in the life of the culture. This is the age of "enlightenment" (Socrates and Rousseau) in which the traditional code is now subjected to a rigorous questioning, although it is still powerful as a religious and creative force. The mathematics characteristic of the culture is now definitely formulated, and the "great conclusive" metaphysical systems are constructed (Plato and Aristotle having their contemporaneous parallel in Goethe and Kant).

But each culture, while exemplifying the laws of growth and decay common to all cultures, is a self-contained unit, talking in a language addressed to itself alone. When it has passed, it leaves us its monuments and its scripts, but the experience which these works symbolized has vanished, so that subsequent cultures inherit a body of rigid symbols to which they are psychically alien—much the way one of Jung's typical extraverts would be alien to a typical introvert. In this sense, ancient Greek is as undecipherable a language as Etruscan, since there is no word in the Greek vocabulary which corresponds, in its cultural background, to the word which we select as its equivalent in any one of our modern languages. Consider, for instance, the difference in content between "man" as one of a race who stole the fire from heaven and "man" as a link in the evolutionary chain. It is not hard to imagine how a work of art arising out of the one attitude could be "alien" to a reader in whom the other attitude was ingrained.

Spengler lays great emphasis upon this cultural subjectivism, and even insists upon the subjective element in natural science. He characterizes the science of any given culture as the conversion of its religion into an irreligious field—such concepts as "force" and "energy," for instance, merely being an altered aspect of the omnipotent and omnipresent God conceived at an earlier stage in the same culture.

The growth of science is also the evidence of a radical change in a culture's evolution. At this stage, the intellectualistic, critical, and irreligious elements of the culture gradually rise to the ascendancy. The emotional certainty of the earlier epochs, when religious, metaphysical, and æsthetic systems were built up spontaneously, is now past. The culture becomes a civilization. "In the one period life *reveals* itself, the other has life as its *object.*" In place of the city we have the metropolis, and the "ethical-practical tendencies of an irreligious and unmetaphysical cosmopolitanism." Winter, thereby, is upon us. Hellenistic-Roman Stoicism after 200—returning to our concept of the contemporaneous — is paralleled by ethical socialism after 1900. The theatricality of Pergamene art is matched by Liszt, Berlioz, and Wagner—and Hellenistic painting finds its equivalent in impressionism. The American skyscraper, instead of being looked upon as the evidence of a new "dawn," is interpreted by Spengler as the symptom of decay corresponding to the "architectural display in the cities of the Diadochi."

Spengler thus finds that the high point of our culture has been passed, while we go deeper into the closing period, the era of civilization. With intellectualistic elements predominant, we are no longer fitted for the production of great works of art, but for the technical exploits, for economic, commercial, political, and imperialistic activities. We are, like Rome, which was the civilization of the Greek culture, ordained to be superior as road-builders and inferior as artists. And by his doctrine of cultural subjectivism, even those great works of art which our culture in its more youthful and vigorous stages produced as the symbolization of Western-European experience will become alien as this experience itself recedes before the rise of other cultures having other modes of experience to symbolize.

In conclusion, then: (*a*) Even the greatest works of art are couched, not in the language of "mankind," but in the language of a specific cultural tradition, and the loss of the tradition is like the loss of the dictionary; and (*b*) since art is inevitably inferior in an era of civilization, we are invited to abandon all hope of further artistic excellence in our cultural cycle.

Let us consider first Spengler's subjectivist argument. In discussing each cultural cycle, he finds some dominant trait which characterizes the entire mode of experience peculiar to the culture. Arabic culture, for instance, is "Magian," our own is "Faustian," and the Græco-Roman is "Apollonian." He then shows how these dominant traits manifest themselves in all the various aspects of a culture's "behavior." The Apollonian trait can be expanded as a sense of the "pure present," a concrete "thisness and hereness," which is to be found equally in the repose of the Greek temple, the "corporeality" of Greek mathematics, and the Greek indifference to time (the Greeks had no system of chronological reckoning comparable to our method of dating from the birth of Christ). The same attitude naturally resulted in the development of sculpture into a major art. In contrast, Faustian culture has a pronounced historic sense, a mathematics of function and time, an "aspiring" architecture; and it has developed music into a major art. In painting, the "corporeal" mentality of the Greeks led to the exclusion of sky-blue as a color, and the disinterest in perspective; while the Faustian culture, with its feeling for distance, showed a marked preference for this very blue, and developed perspective exhaustively. Spengler considers this as evidence of totally different subjective states; yet could it not, as well, be used to indicate a very fundamental kind of similarity? If blue and perspective are employed by the Faustian for the same reason that they are rejected by the Apollonian, does not this argue a common basis of choice? It is to grant, categorically, that blue and perspective symbolize for both cultures a sense of distance. A genuinely subjective difference between cultures would be undetectable, for it would involve a situation in which the symbols could be employed with directly opposite content. Blue and perspective could then, for the Greek, mean pure present; and we could have formed the Greek temple, rather than the Gothic cathedral, as our symbol of aspiration. The æsthetic symbols of an alien culture could give us no clue as to the mode of experience behind them.

Furthermore, why should Spengler stop at cultural subjectivism? Why not accept epochal subjectivism as well? If a difference in the traits of a culture involves a difference in the content of its expressionistic symbols, does not his division of a culture into seasons indicate that each season symbolizes a mode of experience peculiar to itself? If a culture speaks a language of its own, then each season has its own dialect of that language. What "vested interests" would this savant save who would so willingly sacrifice an entire culture?

The fact is that epochal subjectivism would interfere with his two major conclusions: cultural subjectivism and æsthetic defeatism. Spengler's division into spring, summer, autumn, and winter is at bottom the formulation of four subjective types, four typical modes of experience which occur in each cultural cycle. Thus, subjectivity is seen to produce its alliances as well as its estrangements. And contemporeaneous epochs of different cultural cycles might even be considered to have more in common than different epochs of the same culture—our "irreligious and cosmopolitan" winter, for instance, being nearer to the same mode of experience in the Græco-Roman cycle than to its own "rural and intuitive" spring. At least, there is more of Apuleius than of Beowulf in the modern *Weltanschauung*. Epochal subjectivity, looked upon in this way, would tend to counteract the estrangements of cultural subjectivity. Cultural subjectivity would not be an *absolute* condition, but an *approximate* one—and the modes of experience in different eras of the world's history would be capable of an approach towards identity.

Epochal subjectivity, furthermore, would constitute a sanction of the modern artist. It would force us to recognize that winter, purely by being a different mode of experience from spring, summer, or autumn, is categorically entitled to symbolize this mode of experience in art. For we must remember that Spengler is applying the Hegelian concept of the *Zeitgeist*. He holds that every age has its particular character, which is manifested in all its activities. There is an *Urphenomen*, a kind of Reality *x*, a "time-spirit"—each specific activity of an age being a different mode of this time-spirit. As Pater once expressed the same idea: "In every age there is a peculiar *ensemble* of conditions which determines a common character in every product of that age, in business and art, in fashion and speculation, in religion and manners, in men's very faces." One might explain this *ensemble* or consistency (if there is such) in behavioristic terms as the result of mutual interaction, since certain attitudes developed in art can be converted into their equivalents in engineering, business, athletics, marriage customs, etc., while each of these in turn can similarly affect the others. Spengler prefers to discuss the matter in his vocabulary of metaphysical mysticism — whence the *Zeitgeist* concept which has made his entire project seem malapropos to more realistic thinkers. But whether one consider the consistency of an age as the manifold manifestation of a time-spirit or as the result of mutual interaction among all our modes of thinking, feeling, and acting, the fact remains that the entire concept places all manifestations of the age upon the same level: any activity, that is, be it intellectual, emotional, practical, or what not, is *symbolic* of the era in which it takes place.

The noteworthy point is: How does Spengler, out of his

system, draw the conclusion that modern art must be "inferior"? Inferior to what? Inferior to the art of "spring," or "summer," or "autumn"? But spring art was a manifestation of the spring era, and thus why not winter art for a winter era? There is no question of superiority or inferiority here— the only problem Spengler's system equips him to discuss is not a matter of "excellence," but of the "symbolic" or the "representative." Which is "better"—a left shoe for a left foot or a right shoe for a right foot? There is no criterion of comparative excellence in his scheme of the symbolic or representative. He can ask only that a work of art typify the characteristics of the era out of which it arises. His logical machinery provides no step beyond the observation that in spring we must have the symbolizations of spring and in winter the symbolizations of winter. To emerge with a judgment in such a case would be like concluding, after an explanation of the earth's seasons as being caused by the planet's revolution about the sun, "therefore winter is 'inferior' to summer."

That art is beset by questions of method is undeniable. That much of our best art today has an "intellectual" aspect seems equally well established. That we are exposed to many conflicting influences, that tentatives have in many instances replaced canons, that our culture is no longer "thoroughbred"—all such can be admitted. In the mere listing of such issues, however, we must realize how much better "fitted" are our contemporaries for dealing with them than were the writers of the "rural and intuitive" era. The earlier writers omitted many aspects of thinking and feeling which, by Spengler's own schema, have since come to the fore. Their cultural "youth" did not equip them to symbolize the fundamental concerns of our cultural "senectitude."

The fact is that Spengler has loaded the dice against us. His analogy of the seasons contains an implicit judgment.

THE STATUS OF ART

If we but select another analogy, an analogy with the pejorative connotations reversed, the result is entirely different. We might, for instance, instead of accepting his interpretation of the culture-civilization dichotomy, consider the earlier stages of a cultural cycle as periods of upbuilding, of pioneering, of grim, hard-working zealotry. Culture, we could say, struggles and wrestles with its environment and its mental confusions to amass an inheritance which civilization, coming after, has the opportunity to squander and enjoy. When a culture is in full swing, it is not only politically and religiously intolerant, but æsthetically intolerant as well. In Leckey's studies of late Rome, for instance, there is much to indicate that living conditions in this decadent "era of peace," before the new turmoil that came with the growth of Christianity, were in many ways picturesque and delightful. Spengler's whole conception of values contains his conclusions in advance. Which may, it is true, be the predicament of us all—but is more vicious in his case because he masks his personal choice as the inescapable verdict of all history.

III

In times of revolution, it is usually the best features of the old régime that are attacked. Vandals, swarming upon a city, will select the finest monuments to topple and leave inferior things unharmed. It is, perhaps, some such psychology which has led many to bring up art for judgment while the harsh aspects of our civilization awaken them to joyful prophesyings.

Most remarkable of all, however, is the fact that the doctrines of art's ineffectualness have flourished in a period noted for its intense utilization of art. As rapidly as "pure" science became applied science (as technologists, carrying out the possibilities opened up by "pure" scientific speculations, utilized scientific principles for the invention of countless unnecessary commodities) just so fast has "pure" literature become applied literature, to the end of making people want these same commodities. For what is our advertising, what is our "success" fiction in the average commercial magazine, what are our cinematic representations of the "good life," but a vast method of determining the criteria of a nation, and thus its conduct, by the assistance of art? And if, as in modern warfare, the fundamental aspirations of our "pure" scientists are derided, similarly in the use of art to promote a belief in the primary cultural value of material acquisitions, the fundamental aspirations of the "pure" artist are derided. The proper complaint here, however, is not that art has been ineffective, but that a certain brand of art has been only too effective.

Still, we should not be driven by the excesses of our opponents into making too good a case for art. Such was, perhaps, much of the trouble in the first place. One cannot advocate art as a cure for toothache without disclosing the superiority of dentistry. Our program is simply to point out that the criterion of "usefulness" has enjoyed much more prestige than its underlying logic merited. Otherwise the issues are left precisely as vague as we would have them; thus:

No categorical distinction can possibly be made between "effective" and "ineffective" art. The most fanciful, "unreal," romance may stimulate by implication the same attitudes towards our environment as a piece of withering satire attempts explicitly. The rarest work may have more influence upon the shaping of society than a work read by millions. A book, as De Gourmont would say, is alive until the last copy is destroyed. We do not, however, presume to glorify "rare" art at the expense of "popular" art. And it would be unjust to assume that the "minority" interests of today are necessarily the "majority" interests of tomorrow. Minorities are not exclusively "ahead" of their times; they may be "behind" their times, "counter" to their times, "aside" from their times. They can arrogate to themselves no corner on worth. There are some forms of excellence (such as complexity, subtlety, remote inquiry, stylistic rigor) which may limit a book's public as surely as though it were a work on higher mathematics. But where directness, picturesqueness, humor, and power are concerned, such qualities seem to fall easily within the range of a general appeal. We ask only to leave the entire matter vague—to say that a work may be popular and good, popular and bad, unpopular and good, unpopular and bad. It may be widely read and ineffectual, widely read and influential, little read and ineffectual, little read and influential. It may usher in something of great value; it may "keep something alive"; it may represent the concerns of a few people living under exceptional conditions. It may, in fact, do all of these things at different times in its history, or in its action upon different kinds of readers.

We advocate nothing, then, but a return to inconclusiveness. A century of "refutations" is salutary at least in emphasizing the fact that art has not been "refuted." For the rest, the artist's ability to express himself in art would be enough, in most instances, to keep him at his vocation, though he felt it a positive offense against mankind. Art needs nothing by way of "sanction" but the neutralizing of its detractors. It needs no "dignity" beyond the mere zero of not being glibly vilified. To the artist, the belief that the ways of influence are devious and unpredictable, and that "anything can happen," should be sufficient justification for devoting himself to his purely æsthetic problems, solving them according to his lights, and letting all other eventualities take care of themselves.

THOMAS MANN AND
ANDRE GIDE

WHEN Gustav von Aschenbach, the hero of Thomas Mann's *Death in Venice*, was about thirty-five years of age, he was taken ill in Vienna. During the course of a conversation, one keen observer said of him: "You see, Aschenbach has always lived like this," and the speaker contracted the fingers of his left hand into a fist; "never like this," and he let his hand droop comfortably from the arm of a chair. It is with such opening and closing of the hand that this essay is to deal.

In the early writings of both Mann and Gide the characters are exceptional, though always in keeping with our metaphor. Mann's concern is with serious and lonely fellows, deviations from type, who are overburdened with a feeling of divergency from their neighbors. In stories like *Der Bajazzo* the deformations are more mental, but generally the subject is simplified by his imagining characters who are physically extravagant. There is Tobias Mindernickel, whose ill-dressed, gaunt, ungainly figure excites the persecution of all healthy children. He buys a little puppy, and names it Esau. They become inseparable, but one day as Esau leaps for food, it is accidentally wounded by a knife which Tobias is holding, whereupon Tobias nurses his puppy with great tenderness. After some days it is cured, it no longer lies gazing at him with bewildered, suffering eyes, it leaps down from its sick-bed, goes racing about with full delight in its puppyhood, with no thought that it is showing how it no longer needs Tobias' morbid tenderness. It is a cheerful little mutt—and maddened at his loss, Tobias plunges his knife into it again, then forlornly gathers its dying body in his arms. Similarly, there is the little Herr Friedemann, who, humble as he is, can by the course of his story be still further humiliated and, in the very act of taking his life, grovels. Mann also writes of an abnormally fat man, who worships his adulterous wife abjectly, and falls dead of apoplexy at a particularly comical moment, topples like a collapsing building, when he feels the full weight of the indignities which have been heaped upon him. And Piepsam, Herr Gottlob Piepsam, a decayed alcoholic, a victim of life if ever there was one, is insulted as he goes to visit the grave of his wife. On the path to the cemetery he is passed by a boy on a bicycle, the merest child who is too happy to be anything but well-meaning, yet Piepsam resents him and works himself into a fatal rage—the story being told fancifully, even cheerfully. After Piepsam has been bundled off in an ambulance, one feels how brightly the sun is shining.

These outsiders (Mann later took over the word "outsider" from the English) appear under many guises. They watch, they compare themselves with others to their own detriment, they are earnest to the point of self-disgust, and they are weighted with vague responsibilities. In *Tonio Kröger* the concept has matured. Tonio's divergencies are subtler. As a writer, he observes the unliterary with nostalgia. Vacillating by temperament, one might almost say vacillating by profession, he seeks simple people, who form for him a kind of retrogressive ideal. He does not fraternize with them, he spies upon them. A Bohemian, he distrusts Bohemianism. He watches these others, awed by the healthiness, or the ease, of their satisfactions. It is a kind of inverted praising, since he envies them for qualities which he himself has outgrown. And it is melancholy.

Against this earnestness, this non-conforming mind's constant preoccupation with conformity, we find in the early writings of Gide much the same rotten elegance as characterizes Wilde's *The Portrait of Dorian Gray*. Religious thinking is perverted to produce an atmosphere of decay and sin-fulness. There is the Baudelairean tendency to invoke Satan as redeemer. Even in a work as late as *Les Nourritures Ter-restres,* we find a crooked evangelism, calling us to vague and unnatural revelations. These artificial prophecies, with a rhetorical, homiletic accent which Gide has since aban-doned, suggest a kind of morbid Whitmanism. In place of expansion across an unpeopled continent, we have a pilgrimage through old, decaying cities, erotic excitations at the thought of anonymity and freedom among the ruins of other cultures. The hero who cries out to Nathaniel is seeking, not the vigor of health, but the intensity of corrup-tion. The mood, if I understand it correctly, has by now lost much of its immediacy, but in his later works Gide has shown it capable of great readaptation; what we find earlier, in an archaistic terminology, is subsequently transformed into something wholly contemporary.

The most thorough contrast between these writers prob-ably arises from the juxtaposition of Mann's *Death in Venice* and Gide's *The Immoralist.* Gustav von Aschenbach is na-tionally respected as a master of his calling. Parts of his works are even among the prescribed reading of school children. His austerity, his "morality of production," is em-phasized. Aschenbach has clearly erected a structure of exter-nal dignity in keeping with the sobriety, the earnestness, which he has brought to the business of writing. But he is now undergoing a period of enervation. He finds that he cannot tackle his page with the necessary zest. As a purely therapeutic measure, he permits himself a trip to Venice, and here becomes fascinated by a young Polish boy, Tadzio, who is living in the same hotel. In his shy and troubled contem-plation of this boy he finds an absorption which is painful, but imperious. Von Aschenbach remains outwardly the man of dignity honored by his nation—he does not, as I recall, ever exchange a word with this Tadzio, whose freshness, liquidity, immaturity are the sinister counterpart to the desiccation of Aschenbach's declining years. But inwardly he is *notwendig liederlich und Abenteurer des Gefühls*. Necessarily dissolute—an adventurer of the emotions—the words are Mann's, when discussing this book in his *Betrachtungen eines Unpolitischen* years afterwards. We thus find again the notion that the artist faces *by profession* alternatives which are contrary to society. The theme of Aschenbach's gloomy infatuation coëxists with the theme of the plague—and we observe the elderly man's erotic fevers metamorphose gradually into the fevers of incipient cholera. A poignant and inventive passage describing his cosmetic treatment at the hands of a barber is followed by Aschenbach's delirious remembrance of lines from the *Phædrus,* wherein Socrates is speaking words of courtship and metaphysics indiscriminately, a merging which Aschenbach makes more pronounced by his own diseased reworking of the Platonic dialogue. A few pages later "a respectably shocked world" receives the news of his death.

The same themes, sickness and sexual vagary, underlie Gide's *The Immoralist*. Michel, after being at the verge of death and being nursed by his bride into vigorous health, subtly drives her to her own grave. Throughout the novel he is profuse in his tenderness, he is almost hysterically attentive to her, but at the same time he is steadily destroying her—and during the final march of her illness he takes her on that savage pilgrimage from city to city which inevitably results in her death. There has been a young Arab on the fringes of this plot, an insolent fellow who first charmed Michel by stealing from his wife. The reader places him unmistakably as a motive in this unpunishable murder. Despite the parallelism between *Death in Venice* and *The Immoralist,* the emphasis is very different. Whereas in Mann we feel most the sense of resistance, of resignation to the point of distress, and Aschenbach's dissolution is matched by a constant straining after self-discipline, in Gide we hear a narrator who relates with more than pride, with something akin to positive advocacy, the unclean details of his life. *"Je vais vous parler longuement de mon corps,"* he opens one chapter in a tone which I sometimes regret he has seen fit to drop from his later work; there is no mistaking its connotations; it is the accent of evangelism, of pleading.

Buddenbrooks and *Lafcadio's Adventure* do not fall in corresponding stages of their authors' developments. *Buddenbrooks,* a remarkably comprehensive realistic novel of life in North Germany, comes much earlier. But the same contrast in attitude is apparent. We might interpret *Buddenbrooks* as having the theme of *Tonio Kröger* greatly subtilized and ramified. This "fall of a family" through four generations is also the "growth of an artist" through four generations. What is lost in health and moral certitude is gained in questioning and conscientiousness, in social and æsthetic sensitiveness, until we arrive at little Hanno the musician, who, like Aschenbach, finally mingles inspiration with disease, as we watch his improvisations become the first symptoms of the typhoid fever that is to result in his death. In *Lafcadio's Adventure,* however, we meet with a brilliant type of villainy, an "æsthetic criminal" who commits crimes for pure love of the art. The character of Lafcadio is perhaps Gide's most remarkable discovery. It suggests a merging of Stendhal's Julien Sorel with those criminals of Dostoevsky whose transgressions are inexplicable from the standpoint of utilitarian purpose.

In *Lafcadio's Adventure* Gide makes a notable change in nomenclature, recasting his "corruption" in more characteristically contemporary moulds of thought. The transgressions have become "secular," advancing from sin to crime. If theology remains, it is relegated to a more superficial function; it becomes background, the story being built about a swindle whereby certain picturesque crooks fleece Catholic pietists. Lafcadio, who remembers five uncles but no father, has placed villainy on a distinguished but difficult plane. The author endows him with accomplishments somewhat lavishly, perhaps even a bit credulously; he seems eager that our sympathies be with this experimenter in crime, who can look upon kindly and vicious acts as almost interchangeable:

"The old woman with the little white cloud above her head, who pointed to it and said: 'It won't rain today!' that poor shriveled old woman whose sack I carried on my shoulders" (he had followed his fancy of traveling on foot for four days across the Apennines, between Bologna and Florence, and had slept a night at Covigliajo) "and whom I kissed when we got to the top of the hill . . . one of what the *curé* of Covigliajo would have called my 'good actions'. I could just as easily have throttled her—my hand would have been as steady—when I felt her dirty wrinkled skin beneath my fingers. . . . Ah! how caressingly she stroked and dusted my coat collar and said *'figlio mio! carino!'* . . . I wonder what made my joy so intense when afterwards—I was still in a sweat—I lay down on the moss—not smoking though— in the shade of that big chestnut-tree. I felt as though I could have clasped the whole of mankind to my heart in my single embrace—or strangled it, for that matter."

We shall not reconstruct here that gratuitous murder which recommends the hero particularly to our attention when poor Fleurissoire, attracted by this pleasant-seeming lad, chooses to seat himself in the same compartment with him and unknowingly excites Lafcadio to homicidal criticism. Gide exacts a very complex reception on the part of his reader. He asks us to observe a moral outrage committed by a charming scoundrel to whose well-being we are considerably pledged. Fleurissoire is the butt of much injustice in this book, but it is Lafcadio, insolent, despotic, with his mercurial slogan "what would happen if . . ." who earns our suffrage.

The war ends, the mythical post-war period begins, and Thomas Mann issues *The Magic Mountain,* Gide *The Counterfeiters.* Our contrast is by no means imperiled. Mann shows how for seven years, during his illness in the mountains, Hans Castorp has lain exposed to moral questionings. While each day observing his temperature and eating five enormous meals to combat the wastage of his phthisis, he is privileged to hear the grave problems of our culture aired by sparring critics, themselves diseased, who speak with much rhetorical and dialectic finish. In particular, a humanist and a Jesuit altercate for his benefit, until Mynheer Peeperkorn enters (a much grander version of Herr Klöterjahn in the story *Tristan*) and routs them both by his inarticulate vitality. He is life, himself ailing, to be sure, but magnificent and overwhelming while he lasts—and Castorp's melancholy respect for him is, in a matured and complex form, Tonio Kröger's respect for the burghers whom he watched with aloof humility. Castorp has the attitude of a student. Under ordinary circumstances he would probably have been unthinking, but he is made sensitive by his illness and his seven years' elevation above the century. He amasses greater understanding chapter by chapter, or at least learns to play one statement against another—until once more we come to that bewildered fever which marks the close of both *Buddenbrooks* and *Death in Venice*. At the last, as we see him on the battlefield, advancing to the aimless business of slaughter, simplified, regimented, unquestioning, we comprehend his evasion. For years he has been uncertain—he now embraces the arbitrary certainty of war. "Moralism, pessimism, humour"—these three qualities, whose interrelation Mann himself has stressed, are the dominant traits of this momentous novel, a summarizing book, a comprehensive and symbolic work to be included in the world's literature of last wills and testaments.

To turn from *The Magic Mountain* to *The Counterfeiters* is to turn from brooding to shrewdness. Cruelty, malice, sensuality, intrigue—such elements are assiduously welded into an entertaining volume, of much subtle literary satisfaction. The reader of *The Magic Mountain* may have to deal with the fruits of complexity on the part of the author, but he receives them simply. The reader of *The Counterfeiters* finds complexity unresolved—he is not even at liberty to differentiate between the absurd and the beautiful. He is left fluctuant, in great tenuousness of moral values. The book continues Gide's development from sin to crime, and reaffirms his sympathy with deviations from the average ethical stock.

Returning to Aschenbach, ill at the age of thirty-five in Vienna, we find ourselves with correspondences for the closed and opened hand. It seems that Mann, who himself has situated the mainspring of his work in conscientiousness, is like his protagonist Aschenbach, with the hand contracted. And Gide, whose works could readily be taken by the immature or the trivial as invitations to the most unscrupulous kinds of living, who masters an air of suave corruption beyond any possible corrupt act, Gide can be the hand relaxed. *Gewissenhaftigkeit, Einsamkeit*—loneliness, the sense of responsibility—are Mann's words; but as the most distinctive device for Gide, I would quote from his *Journal* the triptych: *"nouveauté, vice, art."*

Our primary purpose, however, in establishing this distinction between the conscientious and the corrupt is to destroy it. One need not read far in the writings of Gide to discover the strong ethical trait which dominates his thinking. Perhaps no other modern writer has quoted the New Testament so frequently, or shown such readiness to settle secular issues by formulas drawn from religion. His critical work on Dostoevsky, with its theological distinction between the psychology of humility and the psychology of humiliation, is throughout an exercise in moral sensitiveness. And his Lafcadio is a mass of categorical imperatives. We learn from entries in his diary how, with the athleticism of an anchorite, he plunges a knife into his side for penance, one thrust "for having beaten Protos at chess," another thrust "for having answered before Protos," four thrusts "for having cried at hearing of Faby's death." Faby was one of his "uncles." Protos was his master in adventure, his accomplished rival, and Lafcadio punished himself, it seems, for not having been disdainful enough to let Protos win. Lafcadio's lamentable conduct might even be derived from an excess of scruples, though these scruples are peculiar to himself.

"I began to feel," Gide has written on this subject in his autobiography, *Si le Grain ne meurt,* "that perhaps all men's obligations were not the same, and that God himself might well abhor the uniformity against which nature protests but towards which the Christian ideal seems to lead us in aiming to bring nature under control. I could concede none but an individual morality, its imperatives sometimes in conflict with those of other moralities. I was persuaded that each person, or at least each one of the elect, had to play a rôle on earth, which was wholly his own and did not resemble any other. And every attempt to submit to a general rule became treason in my eyes, yes, treason which I likened to that great unpardonable sin against the Holy Ghost, since the individual lost his precise, irreplaceable significance, his 'savour'."

We should also consider Gide's *Strait is the Gate,* which constructs a sympathetic idyll out of the perverse rigors of chastity. As Alissa is courted by Jerome, the two progress into a difficult relationship, obscuring their sensual attraction beneath pietistic exaltation. Jerome seeks her patiently and unerringly—and with the vocabulary of nobility she beckons to him while continually delaying the time of their union. At first she can offer logical pretexts for this delay, but as they are one by one removed she retreats behind the subterfuges of her faith, and with the assistance of Biblical quotations, morbidly chosen, she remains to the end difficult, pure, intact, a treasure, while loving Jerome with hysterical effusiveness. From the standpoint of its genesis the book is doubtless a companion piece to *The Immoralist*. Both are perverse studies in the frustration of heterosexual union, the one with the connotations of corruption, the other with connotations of great conscientiousness. When bringing the two together, we see that Alissa's moral sensitiveness was no greater than that of Michel. Similarly we should recall in *The Counterfeiters* the brutal letter which the bastard Bernard Profitendieu writes to his nominal father, a dutifully vicious letter, and the first step, we might say, in the growth of Bernard's affection.

Has not Mann, on the other hand, spoken with fervor of a "sympathy with the abyss," an admitting of the morally chaotic, which he considers not merely the prerogative, but the duty, of the artist? Aschenbach is committed to conflict: whatever policy he decides upon for his conduct, he must continue to entertain disintegrating factors in contemplation. That practical "virtuous" procedure which silences the contrary is not allowed him. He must contain dissolution. In "the repellent, the diseased, the degenerate" Mann situates the ethical. Distinguishing between the moral and the virtuous, he finds that the moralist is "exposed to danger" and "resists no evil." As essential components of art he names "the forbidden, the adventurous, scrutiny, and self-abandonment." Defining sin as doubt, he pleads for sinfulness. His work might be called an epistemology of dignity, for he never relinquishes the love of dignity, and never ceases to make the possession of it difficult.

Mann has defined the problematical as the proper sphere of art ("art is the problematical sphere of the human"). In any event, the problematical is the sphere of his own art. Implicit in his work there is a cult of conflict, a deliberate entertaining of moral vacillation, which could not permit a rigid standard of judgments. He has said that the artist must contain his critic, must recognize the validity of contraries. This attitude would make such simple certainty as moral indignation impossible. It would imply exposure to mutually exclusive codes of conduct, diverse modes of behavior. Æsthetically, as he himself has said, he finds the unification of this attitude in irony, which merges the sympathetic and antipathetic aspects of any subject. Unlike the satirist, the standpoint of the ironist is shifting—he cannot maintain a steady attack—by the standards of military morale he is treacherous; he belittles the things he lives for, and with melancholy praises what he abandons. He is equally tentative towards *Leben,* "life, nature," and *Geist,* "spirit," the intellectual order erected above life. The vigor of the pamphleteer is denied him. To the Rooseveltian mind he is corrosive—wherefore that "sympathy with the abyss" which anyone of rigid criteria, of sure distinctions between the admirable and the reprehensible, must feel as corrupting, and which Mann himself, approaching from the attitude of alien criticism, chose to designate as "dissolute." The ironist is essentially *impure,* even in the chemical sense of purity, since he is divided. He must deprecate his own enthusiasms, and distrust his own resentments. He will unite waveringly, as the components of his attitude, "dignity, repugnance, the problematical, and art."

To the slogan-minded, the ralliers about a flag, the marchers who convert a simple idea into a simple action, he is an "outsider." Yet he must observe them with nostalgia, he must feel a kind of awe for their fertile assurance, even while remaining on the alert to stifle it with irony each time he discovers it growing in unsuspected quarters within himself. It will continue to rise anew, for man has a tremendous fund of certainty—and one will find only too little of Mann's best ironic manner in his essays written during the war, or will find it without its counterpart of melancholy. Yet I grant that the slogans of his opponents were enough to infuriate any subtle man in his position; the temporary disorientation which turned him away from the ironist and towards the pamphleteer is readily understandable. In *The Magic Mountain,* however, the author his recovered from his citizenship to become again the artist. Castorp descends, not to a specific European war, but to regimentation, to the relief, even the suicidal relief, of the slogan-minded. He, the hero, represents the ultimate betrayal of his author's own most serious message. After years of vacillation he seeks the evasion of a monastery, though in these secular days, when the power of theology has dwindled, the dogmatic certainties for which people are burned will more often be those of patriotism, and the equivalent of churchly penance becomes the advance in numbers under arms.

What Mann does with irony, Gide parallels with experimentalism, with curiosity. He views any set code of values with distrust, because it implies the exclusion of other codes. He speculates as to "what would happen if . . ." He is on guard lest the possible be obscured by the real. In his autobiography we find him, characteristically, considering a whole civilization gratuitously different from our own:

"I thought of writing the imaginary history of a people, a nation, with wars, revolutions, changes of administration, typical happenings. . . . I wanted to invent heroes, sovereigns, statesmen, artists, an artistic tradition, an apocryphal literature, explaining and criticizing movements, recounting the evolution of forms, quoting fragments of masterpieces. . . . And all to what purpose? To prove that the history of man could have been different—our habits, morals, customs, tastes, judgments, standards of beauty could have all been different —and yet the humanity of mankind would remain the same."

By recalling *Gulliver's Travels,* we see again how far removed we are from satire. Perhaps, in a much simpler and more lyrical form, Gide did write this book. I refer to *La Symphonie Pastorale,* where he speculates upon a world foreign to him, the world of blindness. He even contrives to forget his own knowledge, as when his blind heroine, trying to meditate her way into the world of sight, surmises that sunlight must be like the humming of a kettle.

Perhaps one may interpret Gide's "corruption" too literally. I do not believe that his work can be evaluated properly unless we go beyond the subject-matter to the underlying principles. His choice of material even implies a certain obscurantism, assuming a sophistication on the part of the reader whereby the reader would not attempt too slavishly to become the acting disciple of his author's speculations. Surely Gide would be the first to admit that we could not build a very convenient society out of Lafcadios, however admirable they are. I should take the specific events in Gide as hardly more than symbols: their parallel in life would not be the enacting of similar events, but the exercising of the complex state of mind which arises from the contemplation of such events with sympathy. To live a life like the life in Gide's books would be to commit under another form the very kind of exclusion which he abhors—Lafcadio is for the pious, he is not for poisoners and forgers. Nor must one, in placing this author's malice, forget his *Travels in the Congo,* with its protests against the systematic injustice meted out to the Negroes at the hands of the concessionaires.[1]

Irony, novelty, experimentalism, vacillation, the cult of

[1] It is doubtful, I grant, whether Gide arrived at his useful position through wholly untrammeled motives. The Olympian result shows

conflict—are not these men trying to make us at home in indecision, are they not trying to humanize the state of doubt? A philosopher has recently written of this new wilderness we now face, a wilderness not of nature, but of social forces. Perhaps there is an evasion, a shirking of responsibility, in becoming certain too quickly, particularly when our certainties involve reversions to an ideology which has the deceptive allurement of tradition. To seek the backing of the past may be as cowardly as to seek the backing of the many, and as flattering to our more trivial needs of conformity. Need people be in haste to rebel against the state of doubt, when doubt has not yet permeated the organs of our body, the processes of our metabolism, the desire for food and companionship, the gratification with sun and water? There is a large reserve of physical unquestioning, and until we find this reserve itself endangered by the humiliation of tentative living and unauthoritative thinking, are we compelled to reach out impetuously for set criteria? Since the body is dogmatic, a generator of belief, society might well be benefited by the corrective of a disintegrating art, which converts each simplicity into a complexity, which ruins the possibility of ready hierarchies, which concerns itself with the problematical, the experimental, and thus by implication works corrosively upon those expansionistic certainties preparing the way for our social cataclysms. An art may be of value purely through preventing a society from becoming too assertively, too hopelessly, itself.

traces of troubled, Orphic beginnings. It seems likely that his concern with homosexuality, and his struggle for its "recognition," early gave him a sense of divergence from the social norms among which he lived, and in time this sense of divergence was trained upon other issues. In seeking, let us say, to defend a practice which society generally considered reprehensible, he came to defend practices which society considered more reprehensible—as a child who resented a cruel father might end by slaying the king.

Could action be destroyed by such an art, this art would
be disastrous. But art can at best serve to make action more
labored. To be sure, so long as we feel the need of certitude,
the state of doubt is discomforting, and by its very prolongation can make for our hysterical retreat into belief, as Hans
Castorp descended from his mountain to the battlefield. But
why could one not come to accept his social wilderness without anguish, utilizing for his self-respect either the irony and
melancholy of Mann, or the curiosity of Gide? In the un-
formed there are opportunities which can be invigorating to
contemplate. One need not suffer under insecurity any more
than an animal suffers from being constantly on the alert
for danger. This state of technical apprehension can be a
norm, and certainly an athletic norm.

No, our fellows want the seasoned stocks and bonds of set
beliefs, and they hope to enrich themselves in these securities
as rapidly as possible. Meanwhile, there is an art, a questioning art, still cluttered with the merest conveniences of thinking, a highly fluctuant thing often turning against istelf and
its own best discoveries. How far it will go, how well it can
maintain its character, I should not venture to calculate.
But working in the traditions of such art are the two conscientious, or corrupt, writers, Thomas Mann and André
Gide. When art is asked to set itself up as *"præceptor pat-
riæ,* haranguing youth in the classical style of virtue, without
shame,"* they remain men who, with considerable literary
endowments, maintain "the Bohemian, the ironic and melancholy, the unattached, the grimly humorous, the innocent,
the childish." They do so, it is true, under a deceptive guise.
They are not Villons, or Baudelaires. Nor will they relinquish
the Villon, the Baudelaire.

See preface, xiii

PROGRAM

Aʀᴛ — "eternal" in so far as it deals with the constants of humanity ("constants of humanity": the recurrent emotions, the fundamental attitudes, the typical experiences).

But art is also historical—a particular mode of adjustment to a particular cluster of conditions. The cluster of conditions is fluctuant (from age to age, from class to class, from person to person) thus calling for changes of emphasis. (Before the flowering of chemistry, for instance, there may have been some value in stressing the heroism of war. A more fitting emphasis now may be the analogy between war and mosquito extermination. Neither aspect is "the truth." Either can be stressed with justice. But a change in the cluster of conditions requires the change of stress.)

Any particular cluster of conditions will involve the recurrent emotions (fear, tenderness, delight, etc.), and fundamental attitudes (belief, cynicism, skepticism, expansiveness, reclusion, etc.); but the particularities of the cluster will require the stressing of some and the slighting of others. (The simplicity and faith needed to construct a particular society may serve badly in the subsequent business of annulling the society's excesses.)

The present Program speculates as to which emotions and attitudes should be stressed, and which slighted, in the æsthetic adjustment to the particular conditions of today.

In contemporary America the distinguishing emergent factor is obviously mechanization, industrialism, as it affects our political institutions, as it alters our way of living, as it makes earlier emphases malapropos or even dangerous ("malapropos or even dangerous"—consider for instance the

107

many social difficulties arising from the doctrine of *laissez-faire,* though the counterpart of this doctrine, self-dependence and individualism, was an adequate adjustment to the conditions of pioneering).

Agrarian–industrial. The agrarians, in so far as their ways of living retain many traits characteristic of the past, will with justice retain the emphases of the past. The industrialized masses, who are living under conditions more definitely "new," will be more amenable to new emphases. (Note the metropolitan tendency to include under the plus-sign of "relaxation" many practices which the agrarians—in so far as they remain agrarians—would tend to include under the minus-sign of "dissipation.")

The artist, who is seeking to adjust a vocabulary to a situation (stressing such ways of feeling as equip one to cope with the situation) is necessarily sensitive to both the surviving and the emergent factors in the situation. The contemporary being an aggregate of survivals and possibilities, the artist wholly awake to the contemporary will embody a mixture of retentions and innovations.

His innovations today must be, in some way, the humanistic or cultural counterpart of the external changes brought about by industrialism, or mechanization. The innovations will stress such emotions and attitudes as favor the acceptance of the changes. ("Acceptance of"—not necessarily "acquiescence to." By acceptance is meant an openness to the factors involved. One may accept a situation in thundering against it. Voltaire accepted. Acceptance is exposure. Whether one builds a wall against the new by reaffirming the old, or seeks by a loosening to incorporate the new, he will be "accepting" in so far as his terminology takes the new into account and gives us an accurate workable attitude towards it.)

Indeterminate position of the artist: His sensitiveness to change must place him at odds with the moral conservatism of the agrarians (who will prefer the partially "unaware" artist, the artist wholly of retentions, the artist free of new emphases). But the industrialist elements likewise will meet his innovations with resistance, insofar as their own values are primarily a survival. The industrialist elements are prepared for the new emphases in that they "need" such (need the orientation of a revised vocabulary, need the implement of an accurate contemporary art to give them appropriate motions and emotions); but their resistance to the new emphases will derive from the force of older emphases already learned. Wherefore the artist, insofar as he is exposed to the whole of the contemporary situation, will budge, rather than flatter, his audience. His cultural innovations must place him at odds with the agrarians (whose way of living retains many important pre-industrialist aspects, and thus justifies their resistance to the "new"); but these same cultural innovations must place him at odds with the industrialized masses who accept their own new procedures simply as a "break-down" of the old and who, even when they do admit cultural innovation, will usually be found to harbor a set of cultural retentions which completely undo it (thus, some industrialist leaders, recognizing that improved methods of production may lead to enforced idleness, admit that their industry may eventually be placed upon a seasonal basis, with even several months a year in which the factories are closed.

But they do not consider the necessary cultural concomitant of such a change. They would meet the rise of technological unemployment by decreasing the hours of labor. Yet they still hold to the blessedness of toil and are in many cases themselves unceasing workers. They retain in thsi respect the mental equipment of the pioneer—who had to "glorify" toil if he was to survive. Under a system where the rise of leisure seems imperative — if we are to avoid the alternations of war and overproduction — they are not equipped for leisure, and at slack times can merely wait, more or less corruptly, with greater or less demoralization, for the resumption of labor.)

Again, since the artist's medium is composed of "survivals," being simply his few additions to a long line, his sensitiveness to many cultural values of the past will generally be greater than that of the masses whose own cultural survivals lead them to resist his "innovations." That is, the man who has indirectly had Elizabethan values made vivid for him (though approaching them as method, he gets a deeper sense of the attitudes behind the method) will probably endow his "survivals" with greater vitality than a person in whom they survive mainly because they have not yet been eradicated. In this particular, the artist's sympathy with pre-industrialist standards may be keener than that of the agrarians themselves (whose code is, in any event, fundamentally vitiated by their envy of industrialist "privileges" and is weakened by a constant bombardment of city influence).

By "innovations," incidentally, is not meant something new under the sun. By innovation is meant simply an emphasis to which the contemporary public is not accustomed. Thus, to a people improvident through excessive hopefulness, the artist who disclosed the cultural value of fear, distrust, or hypochondria would be an innovator. Any "transvaluation of values" is an innovation, though it be a reversion to an earlier value. There could be no more pronounced innovator, by this definition, than a present-day Churchman who would stress the fundamentally anarchistic tenets of primitive Christianity.

Practical–æsthetic. In so far as the conversion of pure science into applied science has made the practical a menace, the æsthetic becomes a means of reclamation. Insofar as mechanization increases the complexity of the social structure (to the point where nothing short of great virtue and great efficiency can make it function without disaster) the æsthetic must serve as anti-mechanization, the corrective of the practical. It is not true that the æsthetic and the practical are necessarily opposed. The terms of one are readily convertible into the terms of the other (consider the barrage of "ideas" needed to prepare a nation for battle; or consider how the most aloof Utopian imaginings can lead people to demand changed policies). Again, the opposition vanishes when a machine is beautiful. Accordingly, to ask that the æsthetic set itself in opposition to the practical is to ask that the æsthetic be one specific brand of the æsthetic. The present essay asks that the æsthetic ally itself with a Program which might be defined roughly as a modernized version of the earlier bourgeois-Bohemian conflict.

Alignment of forces. On the side of the practical: efficiency, prosperity, material acquisitions, increased consumption, "new needs," expansion, higher standards of living, progressive rather than regressive evolution, in short, ubiquitous optimism. Enthusiasm, faith, evangelizing, Christian soldiering, power, energy, sales drives, undeviating certainties, confidence, co-operation, in short, flags and all the jungle vigor that goes with flags. This healthy club-offer we shall give to the practical, which is to replace the "bourgeois" in our modernized version of the bourgeois–Bohemian dichotomy (and surely no one could complain that we have been niggardly in endowing the enemy). On the side of the æsthetic (the Bohemian): inefficiency, indolence, dissipation, vacillation, mockery, distrust, "hypochondria," non-conformity, bad sportsmanship, in short, negativism. Experimentalism, curiosity, risk, dislike of propaganda, dislike of certainty—tentative attitude towards all manners of thinking which reinforce the natural dogmatism of the body. (The certainties of food, shelter, sleep, sex, are enough in themselves to keep a world in turmoil. They should not be reinforced by a set of values which simply project them, disguised but unchanged, into contemporary society, as when we project our love of muscle into a corresponding respect for mental slugging, or project the predatory instincts into an adulation of financial authority.) The practical: patriotism—the æsthetic: treason.

To the Bohemian, or æsthetic, we have relegated a set of qualities which, as so specified, will have few defenders. And their defense is, indeed, difficult and roundabout, with the possible exception of our key-word, "curiosity," though even that is often discredited by companionship with an adjective of ill repute: "idle." (Note how roundabout the defense must ordinarily be: "Indolent." Indolent school children. Beating did little good. They remained indolent. Then it was found that by improving the ventilation one made them less indolent. After which it was found that under a changed curriculum and new methods of instruction many of these school children not only ceased to be indolent but showed an exceptionally keen interest in their studies. So a pandemic of indolent school children might indicate that something is wrong with the school? And the most receptive children might be the ones most depressed by a faulty system? Then might indolence, under certain conditions, be symptomatic of a virtue in the indolent? Such is the roundabout defense for the æsthetic side of the conflict.)

Further defense of the æsthetic, as here defined: the service of the æsthetic in keeping the practical from becoming too hopelessly itself. (There is much usefulness in despair. One who takes out insurance is, to that extent, a hypochondriac. In preparing for imaginary ills we also prepare for real ones.

Greece perished of *Vergötterung* — and by *Verteufelung* the Middle Ages got themselves a long future. Only because there was a flood does the Bible neglect to picture the morbidity of the man who, during many years of gloomy expectancy, built the Ark.) The æsthetic defensible because it could never triumph. Certainties will always arise, impelling men to new intolerances. (Certainty is cheap, it is the easiest thing of which a man is capable. Deprive him of a meal, or bind his arms, or jockey him out of his job — and convictions spring up like Jacks-in-the-box.) Thus, we can defend the æsthetic as anti-practical, anti-industrial, anti-machine because the practical, the industrial, the mechanized is so firmly entrenched. Did distrust kill all believing, did sloth kill all efficiency, then the æsthetic as here defined would be simply suicide. But we may depend upon it that even a world rigorously schooled in doubt will be dogmatical enough. The æsthetic principle as the de-Occidentalizing of the West (a de-Occidentalizing, be it noted, which is justified only while the West remains so thoroughly Occidental; the Orient might well cultivate many of those very tendencies which the Occident should discourage).

The artist — as artist — is not generally concerned with specific political issues. He usually deals with the attitudes, the emphases, in which the choice of some one political or economic policy is implicit, but he need not — as artist — follow the matter through to the full extent. He may sing of pastoral moments on the shores of the Mississippi, nothing more; but if the things he extols there are found to be endangered by the growth of chain stores, his purely pastoral concerns involve by implication the backing of an anti-chain store candidate for President. Thus, a system of æsthetics subsumes a system of politics (and though the artist— *qua* artist—may ignore it, the present Program of critical orientation cannot ignore it). Accordingly, to speculate upon the practical consequences of our "negativistic" æsthetic:

Fascism-democracy. Democracy is coming into disrepute among the practical on the grounds of its "inefficiency." Government by economists, it is hoped, will replace government by politicians. The nation, finding its Legislatures and Congress balked and bungling through the clash of party interests (democracy—system of checks and counter-checks) begins to desire a more "efficient" form of government, with problems of production and distribution handled as they are by the co-ordinating head of a large factory (ideal Fascism—guidance in accordance with economic principles—central authority). Now the practical, who are well endowed with faith, like to assume that the proposed authority will be both benevolent and capable. (Why they make such cautious plans, after this beginning, I do not know—for once you postulate human virtue as the foundation of a system, you are a dullard indeed if you can't make up a thousand schemes for a good society. A society is sound only if it can prosper on its vices, since virtues are by very definition rare and exceptional.) The æsthetic (by our definition—the æsthetic, that is, this particular brand of the æsthetic, the anti-practical) would be driven back to democracy (a system of government based upon the fear that central authority becomes bad authority—democracy, organized distrust, "protest made easy," a babble of discordant voices, a colossal getting in one's own way—democracy, now endangered by the apostles of hope who would attack it for its "inefficiency," whereas inefficiency is the one thing it has in its favor).

"If the flowering of industrialism requires vast efficiency, vast ingenuity, and the promotion of virtue to a position of authority," says the distrusting, the æsthetic (the democrat), "then let the flower of industrialism wither." If there is some force to be controlled, we can control it either by perfecting the means of control or by impairing the force to be controlled. The Fascists, the hopeful, the propounders of business culture, believe that the future lies in perfecting the means of control. The democrat, the negativist, the man who thinks of powers as something to be "fought," has no hope in perfection—as the "opposition," his nearest approach to a doctrine is the doctrine of interference. (There is no absolute truth, he says, but there is the cancellation of errors: and even if you reduced people to the unlearned zero of their origins, they would still have the ample troublous plus-signs of their physiological demands; for while there is life, things are hopeless.) And so to recapitulate: the æsthetic would seek to discourage the most stimulating values of the practical, would seek—by wit, by fancy, by anathema, by versatility—to throw into confusion the code which underlies commercial enterprise, industrial competition, the "heroism" of economic warfare; would seek to endanger the basic props of industry.

"Discourage" industry? We have seen how industry, alas! can be only too drastically discouraged. And if one would undermine the basic props of industry, he must be sure that the masses are not crushed in the fall. It is obvious that industry cannot be discouraged without the spread of misery among millions unless the democrats take to the generous spending of the industrialists' fortunes. The redistribution of wealth by some means—nationalization, or income and inheritance taxes, or some such—is an important political and economic implication of an "anti-industrial" æsthetic. One cannot safely discourage industry unless the principle of the "dole" is applied on so vast a scale that the terror of joblessness is eliminated. The dole as the "norm"—thus, a society which seeks to construct the amenities of living not upon "good times," but upon "bad times." The dole—levied out of excess wealth—guaranteeing to everyone an irreducible minimum upon which to subsist. Particularly among the lower

forms of employment it should eliminate competitive zest—
especially if it were accompanied by such a change in ideology that no stigma were attachable to the receiving of a
government stipend.

Unemployment–leisure. Under the increasing productivity
of machinery, society will eventually face a choice between
the menace (unemployment) and the amenity (leisure). The
dole, subtracted from the excess profits of industry, is the
only means of avoiding the menace. The advance of mechanization makes the radical reduction of total working hours
not merely a privilege, but a necessity. Hence the dilemma,
solvable on both horns by the dole: as the total working
hours diminish, the wage for the working hour must increase,
which amounts to saying that eventually a man must be
paid for his leisure; or if the total working hours are to be
maintained by the stimulation of new needs, the employers
must give copiously of their profits in order that the employees may buy. In America the need of a vast tax upon
excess profits has been obscured by the fact that much of
the excess profits has been reinvested in foreign bonds which
have since partially or wholly depreciated. If industry is
stimulated by a foreign loan, this loan is simply, to the
extent of the bonds' depreciation, a disguised tax on excess
profits used to stimulate further buying. Thus, we advocate
the anti-industrialist program not as mere demagogic van-
dalism, but as the facing of a necessity, which necessity is:
technological unemployment must be made technological
leisure; leisure—as we learn from capitalism itself—must be
subsidized from excess profits; the appropriation of excess
profits, in whatever form this process takes, constitutes the
"dole"; and if the dole is to be accepted without demoralization, we must so alter the current "philosophy" of ambition,
work, earnings, economic glory, that the recipients of the

dole can receive it, not as paupers, but as slave owners (slave owners, living off the labor of the automata; I recall the laborer who stood, his arms crossed like Napoleon, while an obedient cement-mixer dumped a load into his wheel-barrow).

Overproduction–underconsumption. If we remove the discrepancy between production and consumption by lowering production, the people who are put out of work must be paid for their leisure. And to remove the discrepancy by increasing consumption, we must give the employees the employers' profits to buy with. Ergo: either way, the dole.

Confusion of terms: Concerning the political alignment in such attacks upon industry as we propose: the industrialists, who are responsible for radical alterations in our ways of living, are known politically and economically as "conservatives." (During the Reconstruction the industrialist faction of the Republican Party was, accurately, termed the Radicals.) The agrarian elements, which come nearest to retaining pre-industrialist modes of living and thinking, are known politically and economically as liberal, or Progressive. (Industrialism has spread to such an extent that industrial radicalism has become the "norm," and is enshrined as conservatism. And since it is to the interest of the agrarians that industrialist hegemony be checked, the measures of governmental control they advocate become "radical.")

Paradox: politically, agrarian conservatism is the equivalent of anti-industrialist radicalism. Wherefore the agrarians, whose moral practices are quite different from those of the industrialized masses (as in matters of alcohol, Sunday recreation, easy divorce) are nonetheless close to these masses in their attempts to curb the powers of the industrialist leaders. Thus it is among the farmers, the only surviving American conservatives, that a radical anti-industrialist movement must be fostered.[1] Hence more confusion in our Program: for the political implications of the æsthetic as here defined would involve a political alignment with the agrarians; yet morally the artist, as an innovator, will experiment to formulate the cultural counterpart to industrialism (manifesting, for instance, a tendency towards the irreligiosity of the city); and this cultural counterpart will involve the destruction of values—such as the cluster of emphases stimulating commercial ambition—which are now shared by agrarian and industrialist elements alike.

Then the artist will *strive assiduously* to fit the world for *leisure?* There is no inconsistency here—for art remains an "inefficient" business, hence one to which the earlier philosophy of toil can still be applied. Again, an important aspect of the artist's "efficiency" resides not in an accumulation of products, but in a ceaseless indwelling, a patient process of becoming expert in himself *(numquam minus otiosus, quam cum esset otiosus)*. Furthermore, be it noted that such use of the "æsthetic" does not rely upon virtue. It would found a society upon vices. Politically it would observe the principle of democratic distrust (government through conflict of selfish interests) over against the Fascist hopefulness (centralization of *benevolent* authority). And so far as the "good work" of the artists is concerned—though it should, by our way of reasoning, be "good" in its results, it would certainly require no moral "goodness" on the part of the doers. The policy would, for one thing, gratify the self-importance of the artist. Again, being primarily a process of disintegration, of making propaganda difficult, of fostering intellectual dis-

[1] That is, there is a likelihood of "rebellion" in America only if there is some conservative group whose interests make it the equivalent of a radical group. Ideologically conservative—functionally radical.

trust, it would require no exceptional efforts on the part of the artist, as the absurdities and disasters of contemporary society are prevalent enough. In fact, many an artist who would turn from my suggestions with loathing is already, in his own way, carrying them into effect, though he be doing no more than to provide his readers with naïve dreams of "escape" (for people have gone too long with the glib psychoanalytic assumption that an art of "escape" promotes acquiescence. It may, as easily, assist a reader to clarify his dislike of the environment in which he is placed). The artist can, as we have said, become "subversive" by merely singing, in all innocence, of respite by the Mississippi. It takes no heroism, or even awareness, for him to contribute his part in this "revolution." It is easy to exploit the miseries of a system which, in encouraging the basic certainties of power, has caused so many physiological needs to be perverted in so many people. The artist requires but the technical virtue of craftsmanship which, we know, is not rare like the moral virtues, but usually arises wherever a man has some authority over the choice and the disposition of his tasks and where he himself makes the complete object.

Recapitulation: The machine being strong enough to take care of itself, let us not pamper it by a "philosophy" of efficiency which makes overproduction a menace (when overproduction should, obviously, be man's greatest cause for comfort). Let us attempt to bring to the fore such "Bohemian" qualities as destroy great practical enterprise. (When in Rome, do as the Greeks — when in Europe, do as the Chinese.) Let us reaffirm democracy (government by interference, by distrust) over against Fascism (regulation by a "benevolent" central authority—society based upon virtue, which is too flimsy a base, since it requires [a] that people be too consistently virtuous, [b] that the virtuous be also the capable, and [*c*] that the virtuous-capable be the persons who rise to authority). "But," say the practical, "interference, bad co-ordination, is the essential cause of our difficulties today; the 'system' requires its elimination." To which the æsthetic, as here defined, makes answer: "When a system becomes so complex that it requires a high degree of perfection for its survival, when it can't provide a civilized living by shoddy, unintelligent, lethargic methods, then mankind had better change the system for a system which can provide a civilized living by shoddy, unintelligent, lethargic methods." When inefficiency becomes a danger, we should so alter the system that inefficiency ceases to be a danger. This change we see in a shift of emphasis from "good times" to "bad times" as the norm. In loss of faith, we say, resides the kind of vague, bungling adjustment which a society seems capable of making with some degree of success. Such an adjustment would require the organized "pauperization" of the masses (by the normalization of the dole, a government stipend below which a man could not fall). The profit motive could be left to the enterprising commercialist, but he would be heavily taxed for his enterprise (by not being permitted, let us say, to keep for himself any larger fortune than a million men could spend).

Purpose? Efficiency breeds but the necessity of more efficiency. It requires not only a mounting expenditure of eternal vigilance, but a nicety of adjustment whereby the eternally vigilant are also the authoritative. But above all, one must accept the undeniable fact that technological efficiency has become too much like psychological inefficiency. It has, paradoxically, by projecting our "jungle ways" into their simple civilized equivalent, brought man to a stage where the proper exercise of his most gratifying jungle ways is sadly restricted. "Efficiency" was required to develop the machine. "Inefficiency" is required as the counter-principle to prevent the machine from becoming too imperious and forcing us into social complexities which require exceptional delicacy of adjustment. The "Bohemian," the "æsthetic," as here defined, relegates enterprise to such inquiries and imaginings as serve to "corrode" the practical—it is concerned with such intellectual vagabondage, such aspects of "irresponsibility," as constitute a grave interference with the cultural code behind our contemporary economic ambitiousness.

Finally: This Program would not, let it be repeated, sum up the absolute, unchanging purposes of the æsthetic. It would define the function of the æsthetic as effecting an adjustment to one particular cluster of conditions, at this particular time in history. As for the "eternal" aspect of such art, however, I do not see that it would be in any way endangered by so specific a Program. The artist who wrote a novel called *Vive the Dole* would, most probably, find that his work died with the death of the specific situation for which it was written. But an artist who dealt simply with emotions and attitudes in their broader aspects (leaving the specific political and economic considerations to take care of themselves) would not find his work impaired by the rise of new conditions. For though the state of society may be such, at a certain time, that certain emotions and attitudes prevail, and the state of society may so change that other emotions and attitudes come to prevail, the gamut of human emotions and attitudes is neither increased nor diminished. Thus can one, out of the particularities of his times, write for other times —since the "gravitational pull" of his contemporary situations will draw him repeatedly to certain emphases, thus making him expert in such emphases as are less exercised in other eras. The cluster of conditions may, for instance, make a man's whole output a song of despair; a later age may, with a kindlier cluster of conditions, feel no such need for this particular emphasis; but in every age there will be a moment in every man's life when he is, for the time at least, routed—and the earlier "expert," who lived all his life with such considerations, and thus became exceptionally adept in dealing with them, will be the writer for this gloomy reader's present ill-starred hour.

LEXICON RHETORICÆ

BEING A CODIFICATION, AMPLIFICATION, AND CORRECTION
OF THE TWO ESSAYS, "PSYCHOLOGY AND FORM"
AND "THE POETIC PROCESS"

THE PRESENT essay attempts to define the principles underlying the appeal of literature. By literature we mean *Working def. of Lit.*
written or spoken words. Primarily we are concerned with
literature as art, that is, literature designed for the express
purpose of arousing emotions. But sometimes literature so
designed fails to arouse emotions — and words said purely
by way of explanation may have an unintended emotional
effect of considerable magnitude. A discussion of effectiveness
in literature should be able to include unintended effects as
well as intended ones. Also, such a discussion will be diag-
nostic rather than hortatory: it will be more concerned with
how effects are produced than with *what effects should be
produced.*

As far as possible, we shall proceed simply by definition
and example. We propose: to analyze the five aspects of *Outline of essay*
form (The Nature of Form); to show how these forms are
implicit in subject-matter (The Individuation of Forms); to
discuss subject-matter and forms as combined in the Symbol
(Patterns of Experience); to distinguish between the scientific formulation of experience and the poet's formulation of
experience (Ritual); and to consider the problems of literary
excellence (Permanence, Universality, Perfection). Then,
having completed our Lexicon, we propose to examine certain critical issues of the past and of the present, testing our
terms as equipment for the discussion of these issues.

COUNTER-STATEMENT

THE NATURE OF FORM

1. *Form* in literature is an arousing and fulfillment of desires. A work has form in so far as one part of it leads a reader to anticipate another part, to be gratified by the sequence. The five aspects of form may be discussed as progressive form (subdivided into syllogistic and qualitative progression), repetitive form, conventional form, and minor or incidental forms.

2. *Syllogistic progression* is the form of a perfectly conducted argument, advancing step by step. It is the form of a mystery story, where everything falls together, as in a story of ratiocination by Poe. It is the form of a demonstration in Euclid. To go from A to E through stages B, C, and D is to obtain such form. We call it syllogistic because, given certain things, certain things must follow, the premises forcing the conclusion. In so far as the audience, from its acquaintance with the premises, feels the rightness of the conclusion, the work is formal. The arrows of our desires are turned in a certain direction, and the plot follows the direction of the arrows. The peripety, or reversal of the situation, discussed by Aristotle, is obviously one of the keenest manifestations of syllogistic progression. In the course of a single scene, the poet reverses the audience's expectations—as in the third act of *Julius Cæsar,* where Brutus' speech before the mob prepares us for his exoneration, but the speech of Antony immediately after prepares us for his downfall.

3. *Qualitative progression,* the other aspect of progressive form, is subtler. Instead of one incident in the plot preparing us for some other possible incident of plot (as Macbeth's murder of Duncan prepares us for the dying of Macbeth),

124

the presence of one quality prepares us for the introduction of another (the grotesque seriousness of the murder scene preparing us for the grotesque buffoonery of the porter scene). In T. S. Eliot's *The Waste Land,* the step from "Ta ta. Goonight. Goonight" to "Good night, ladies, good night, sweet ladies" is a qualitative progression. In Malcolm Cowley's sonnet *Mine No. 6* there is a similar kind of qualitative progression, as we turn from the octave's description of a dismal landscape ("the blackened stumps, the ulcerated hill") to the sestet's "Beauty, perfection, I have loved you fiercely." Such progressions are qualitative rather than syllogistic as they lack the pronounced anticipatory nature of the syllogistic progression. We are prepared less to demand a certain qualitative progression than to recognize its rightness after the event. We are put into a state of mind which another state of mind can appropriately follow.

4. *Repetitive form* is the consistent maintaining of a principle under new guises. It is restatement of the same thing in different ways. Thus, in so far as each detail of Gulliver's life among the Lilliputians is a new exemplification of the discrepancy in size between Gulliver and the Lilliputians, Swift is using repetitive form. A succession of images, each of them regiving the same lyric mood; a character repeating his identity, his "number," under changing situations; the sustaining of an attitude, as in satire; the rhythmic regularity of blank verse; the rhyme scheme of *terza rima*—these are all aspects of repetitive form. By a varying number of details, the reader is led to feel more or less consciously the principle underlying them—he then requires that this principle be observed in the giving of further details. Repetitive form, the restatement of a theme by new details, is basic to any work of art, or to any other kind of orientation, for that matter. It is our only method of "talking on the subject."

5. *Conventional form* involves to some degree the appeal of form *as form*. Progressive, repetitive, and minor forms, may be effective even though the reader has no awareness of their formality. But when a form appeals as form, we designate it as conventional form. Any form can become conventional, and be sought for itself—whether it be as complex as the Greek tragedy or as compact as the sonnet. The invocation to the Muses; the theophany in a play of Euripedes; the processional and recessional of the Episcopalian choir; the ensemble before the front drop at the close of a burlesque show; the exordium in Greek-Roman oratory; the Sapphic ode; the triolet—these are all examples of conventional forms having varying degrees of validity today. Perhaps even the Jew-and-the-Irishman of the Broadway stage is an instance of repetitive form grown into conventional form. Poets who write beginnings *as beginnings* and endings *as endings* show the appeal of conventional form. Thus, in Milton's *Lycidas* we start distinctly with the sense of introduction ("Yet once more, O ye laurels, and once more . . .") and the poem is brought to its dextrous gliding close by the stanza, clearly an ending: "And now the sun had dropped behind the hills, And now had dropped into the western bay. . . ." But Mother Goose, throwing formal appeal into relief through "nonsense," offers us the clearest instance of conventional form, a "pure" beginning and "pure" end:

> "I'll tell you a story of Jack O'Norey
> And now my story's begun;
> I'll tell you another about his brother
> And now my story is done."

We might note, in conventional form, the element of "categorical expectancy." That is, whereas the anticipations and gratifications of progressive and repetitive form arise *during*

[handwritten marginalia: Adherence to Conventions]

the process of reading, the expectations of conventional form may be *anterior to* the reading. If one sets out to read a sonnet, regardless of what the sonnet is to say he makes certain formal demands to which the poem must acquiesce. And similarly, the final Beethoven rejoicing of a Beethoven finale becomes a "categorical expectation" of the symphony. The audience "awaits" it before the first bar of the music has been played. And one may, even before opening a novel, look forward to an opening passage which will proclaim itself an opening.

6. *Minor or incidental forms.* When analyzing a work of any length, we may find it bristling with minor or incidental forms—such as metaphor, paradox, disclosure, reversal, contraction, expansion, bathos, apostrophe, series, chiasmus—which can be discussed as formal events in themselves. Their effect partially depends upon their function in the whole, yet they manifest sufficient evidences of episodic distinctness to bear consideration apart from their context. Thus a paradox, by carrying an argument one step forward, may have its use as progressive form; and by its continuation of a certain theme may have its use as repetitive form—yet it may be so formally complete in itself that the reader will memorize it as an event valid apart from its setting. A monologue by Shakespeare can be detached from its context and recited with enjoyment because, however integrally it contributes to the whole of which it is a part, it is also an independent curve of plot enclosed by its own beginning and end. The incident of Hamlet's offering the pipes to Guildenstern is a perfect instance of minor form. Euripides, when bringing a messenger upon the stage, would write him a speech which, in its obedience to the rhetorical laws of the times, was a separate miniature form. Edmund Burke sought to give each paragraph a structure as a paragraph, making it a growth,

yet so confining it to one aspect of his subject that the closing sentence of the paragraph could serve as the logical complement to the opening one. Frequently, in the novel, an individual chapter is distinguished by its progress as a chapter, and not solely by its function in the whole. The Elizabethan drama generally has a profusion of minor forms.

7. *Interrelation of forms.* Progressive, repetitive, and conventional and minor forms necessarily overlap. A specific event in the plot will not be exclusively classifiable under one head—as it should not, since in so organic a thing as a work of art we could not expect to find any principle functioning in isolation from the others. Should we call the aphoristic couplet of the age of Pope repetitive form or conventional form? A closing scene may be syllogistic in that its particular events mark the dramatic conclusion of the dramatic premises; qualitative in that it exemplifies some mood made desirable by the preceding matter; repetitive in that the characters once again proclaim their identity; conventional in that it has about it something categorically terminal, as a farewell or death; and minor or incidental in that it contains a speech displaying a structural rise, development, and fall independently of its context. Perhaps the lines in *Othello,* beginning "Soft you, a word or two before you go," and ending "Seized by the throat the uncircumcised dog and smote him thus (*stabs himself*)" well exemplify the vigorous presence of all five aspects of form, as this suicide is the logical outcome of his predicament (syllogistic progression); it fits the general mood of gloomy forebodings which has fallen upon us (qualitative progression); the speech has about it that impetuosity and picturesqueness we have learned to associate with Othello (repetitive form); it is very decidedly a conclusion (conventional form), and in its development it is a tiny plot in itself (minor form). The close of the *Odyssey*

strongly combines syllogistic and qualitative progression. Ulysses' vengeance upon the suitors is the logical outcome of their conduct during his absence—and by the time it occurs, the reader is so incensed with them that he exults vindictively in their destruction. In most cases, we can find some aspects of form predominant, with others tenuous to the point of imperceptibility. Keats's "Ode to a Nightingale" is a striking instance of repetitive form; its successive stanzas take up various aspects of the mood, the *status evanescentiæ,* almost as schematically as a lawyer's brief; but of syllogistic form there is barely a trace. . . . As, in musical theory, one chord is capable of various analyses, so in literature the appeal of one event may be explained by various principles. The important thing is not to confine the explanation to *one* principle, but to formulate sufficient principles to make an explanation possible. However, though the five aspects of form can merge into one another, or can be present in varying degrees, no other terms should be required in an analysis of formal functionings.

8. *Conflict of forms.* If the various formal principles can intermingle, they can also conflict. An artist may create a character which, by the logic of the fiction, should be destroyed; but he may also have made this character so appealing that the audience wholly desires the character's salvation. Here would be a conflict between syllogistic and qualitative progression. Or he may depict a wicked character who, if the plot is to work correctly, must suddenly "reform," thereby violating repetitive form in the interests of syllogistic progression. To give a maximum sense of reality he may, like Stendhal, attempt to make sentences totally imperceptible as sentences, attempt to make the reader slip over them with no other feeling than their continuity (major progression here involving the atrophy of minor forms). Or conventional

form may interfere with repetitive form (as when the drama, in developing from feudal to bourgeois subjects, chose "humbler" themes and characters, yet long retained the ceremonial diction of the earlier dignified period); and conversely, if we today were to attempt regaining some of these earlier ceremonial effects, by writing a play entirely in a ceremonial style, we should be using the appeal of repetitive form, but we should risk violating a contemporary canon of conventional form, since the non-ceremonial, the "domestic" dialogue, is now categorically expected.

9. *Rhythm, Rhyme.* Rhythm and rhyme being formal, their appeal is to be explained within the terms already given. Rhyme usually accentuates the repetitive principle of art (in so far as one rhyme determines our expectation of another, and in so far as the rhyme-scheme in one stanza determines our expectation of its continuance in another). Its appeal is the appeal of progressive form in so far as the poet gets his effects by first establishing, and then altering, a rhyme-scheme. In the ballade, triolet, etc., it can appeal as conventional form.

That verse rhythm can be largely explained as repetitive form is obvious, blank verse for instance being the constant recurrence of iambs with changing vowel and consonantal combinations (it is repetitive form in that it very distinctly sets up and gratifies a constancy of expectations; the reader "comes to rely" upon the rhythmic design after sufficient "coördinates of direction" have been received by him; the regularity of the design establishes conditions of response in the body, and the continuance of the design becomes an "obedience" to these same conditions). Rhythm appeals as conventional form in so far as specific awareness of the rhythmic pattern is involved in our enjoyment (as when the Sapphic meter is used in English, or when we turn from a pentameter sonnet in English to a hexameter sonnet in French). It can sometimes be said to appeal by qualitative progression, as when the poet, having established a pronounced rhythmic pattern, introduces a variant. Such a variant appeals as qualitative progression to the extent that it provides a "relief from the monotony" of its regular surroundings, to the extent that its appeal depends upon the previous establishment of the constant out of which it arises. Rhythm can also appeal as minor form; a peculiarity of the rhythm, for instance, may strikingly reinforce an incidental image (as with the use of spondees when the poet is speaking of something heavy).

In the matter of prose rhythms, the nature of the expectancy is much vaguer. In general the rhythmic unit is larger and more complex than the individual metric foot, often being the group of "scrambled" syllables between two cæsuras. Though the constants of prose rhythm permit a greater range of metric variation than verse rhythms (that is, though in prose much of the metric variability is felt as belonging to the *constant* rather than to the *variation*), a prose stylist does definitely restrict the rhythmic expectations of the reader, as anyone can readily observe by turning from a page of Sir Thomas Browne to a page of Carlyle. However, one must also recall Professor George Saintsbury's distinction: "As the essence of verse-meter is its identity (at least in equivalence) and recurrence, so the essence of prose-rhythm lies in variety and divergence," or again: "Variety of foot arrangement, without definite equivalence, appears to be as much the secret of prose rhythm as uniformity of value, with equivalence or without it, appears to be that of poetic meter." The only thing that seems lacking in this distinction between verse rhythms and prose rhythms is a statement of some principle by which the *variety* in prose rhythms is guided. Perhaps the principle is a principle of logic. An intellectual factor is more strongly involved in the appreciation of prose rhythm than of verse rhythm, as grammatical and ideational relationships figure prominently in the determination of prose balances (a prose balance being the rhythmic differentiation of units which have an intellectual correspondence, by parallelism or antithesis). Thus, to take from Sir Thomas Browne a typical "prose event" (we choose a very simple example from a writer who could afford us many complex ones): the series "pride, vain-glory, and madding vices" is made up of three units which are intellectually equivalent, but their ideational equality coexists with total syllabic asymmetry (the first a monosyllable, the second an amphibrach, the third dochmiac—or one, three, and five syllables, though it is true that in verse scansion the words "and madding vices" would not ordinarily be considered as constituting a single foot). It is also worth noting, as an example of the "intellectual" rhythms in prose, that the third noun is accompanied by an adjective, the second has an adjective engrafted upon it, and the first stands alone; also, the third differs from the other two in number. To consider a slightly more complex example: "Even Scylla, / that thought himself safe in his urn, / could not prevent revenging tongues, / and stones thrown at his monument." Here many complexities of asymmetric balance may be noted: contrast between long subject and short verb; contrast between short verb and long object; the two grammatical components of the subject (noun and clause) are unequal in value, whereas the two main grammatical components of the object ("tongues" and "stones") are equal in value; the modifier in the subject is a clause, whereas the modifiers of the object are participial adjectives; of these two participial adjectives, one ("revenging") is active, precedes its noun, and is of three syllables, but the other ("thrown") is passive, follows its noun, and is monosyllabic; and whereas "revenging" is an unmodified modifier, "thrown" is accompanied by the phrase "at his monument." We might further note that the interval from the beginning to the first cæsura ("Even Scylla") greatly contrasts in length with the interval between the first and second cæsura ("that thought himself safe in his urn"). In two notable respects the third and fourth intervals are surely inferior as prose to the first two. Their iambic quality is concealed with difficulty; there is more than a hint of homœoteleuton ("prevent"—"monument"), which is only suppressed by our placing the cæsura at "tongues" and rigorously avoiding the slightest pause after "prevent." The placing of the cæsura after "tongues," however, has the further advantage of putting "tongues" and "stones" in different intervals, thus once more giving us the asymmetrical by rhythmically separating the logically joined. [We do not imply that one consciously notes such a multitude of dissimilar balances, any more than one consciously notes the complexity of muscular tensions involved in walking—but as there is an undeniable complexity of muscular tensions involved in walking, so there is a multitude of dissimilar balances involved in expert prose. And we are trying to indicate that the rhythmic variations of prose are not haphazard, that their "planfulness" (conscious or unconscious) arises from the fact that the differentiations are based upon logical groupings. That is, by logically relating one part of a sentence to another part of the sentence, the prose writer is led to a formal differentiation of the two related parts (or sometimes, which is *au fond* the same thing, he is led to a pronounced parallelism in the treatment of the related parts). The logical grouping of one part with another serves as the guide to the formal treatment of both (as "planful" differentiation can arise only out of a sense of correspondence). The logical groupings upon which the rhythmic differentiations are based will differ with the individual, not only as to the ways in which he conceives a sentence's relationships, but also as to their number—and much of the "individuality" in a particular prose style could be traced to the number and nature of the author's logical groupings. Some writers, who seek "conversational" rather than "written" effects, apparently conceive of the sentence as a totality; they ignore its internal relationships almost entirely, preferring to make each sentence as homogeneous as a piece of string. By such avoidance of logical grouping they do undeniably obtain a simple fluency which, if one can delight in it sufficiently, makes every page of Johnson a mass of absurdities—but their sentences are, as sentences, uneventful.] The "written" effects of prose seem to stress the progressive rather than the repetitive principle of form, since one part of the sentence is differentiated on the basis of another part (the formal identity of one part awakens in us a response whereby we can be pleased by a formal alteration in another part). But "conversational" rhythm, which is generally experienced "in the lump," as a pervasive monotone rather than as a group of marked internal structures, is—like verse—more closely allied to the repetitive principle. The "conversational" is thus seen to fall halfway between verse-rhythm and prose-rhythm, sharing something of both but lacking the pronounced characteristics of either.

So much for prose rhythm regardless of its subject-matter. We must also recognize the "secondary" aspect of rhythms whereby they can often be explained "at one remove." Thus, a tumultuous character would constantly restate his identity by the use of tumultuous speech (repetitive form), and the rhythm, in so far as it became tumultuous out of sympathy with its subject, would share the repetitive form of the subject. Similarly, it may be discussed as conventional or minor form (as when the author marshals his more aggressive images to mark an ending, and parallels this with a kindred increase in the aggression of his rhythms). In a remote way, all such rhythmic effects may be described as a kind of "onomatopoetic parallelism," since their rhythmic identity would be explainable by the formal nature of the theme to which they are accommodated.

10. *"Significant form."* Though admitting the onomatopoetic correspondence" between form and theme, we must question a quasi-mystical attempt to explain all formal quality as "onomatopoetic" (that is, as an adaptation of sound and rhythm to the peculiarities of the sense). In most cases we find formal designs or contrivances which impart emphasis regardless of their subject. Whatever the theme may be, they add saliency to this theme, the same design serving to make dismalness more dismal or gladness gladder. Thus, if a poet is writing in a quick meter, he may stress one point in his imagery as well as another by the use of spondees; or he may gain emphasis by injecting a burst of tonal saliency, as the aggressive repetition of a certain vowel, into an otherwise harmonious context. In either case the emphasis is gained though there be no discernible onomatopoetic correspondence between the form and the theme (the formal saliency being merely a kind of subtler italics, a mechanism for placing emphasis wherever one chooses, or such "absolute" stressing as comes of pounding the table with one's fist to emphasize either this remark or that). To realize that there is such absolute stressing, one has but to consider the great variety of emotions which can be intensified by climactic arrangement, such arrangement thus being a mere "coefficient of power" which can heighten the saliency of the emotion regardless of what emotion it may be.

As illustration, let us trace one formal contrivance through a set of diverse effects, as it is used in Wilde, Wordsworth, and Racine, and as it appeared by chance in actual life.

Beginning with the last, we may recall a conversation between two children, a boy and a girl. The boy's mind was on one subject, the girl's turned to many subjects, with the result that the two of them were talking at cross-purposes. Pointing to a field beyond the road, the boy asked: "Whose field is that?" The girl answered: "That is Mr. Murdock's field"—and went on to tell where Mr. Murdock lived, how many children he had, when she had last seen these children, which of them she preferred, but the boy interrupted: "What does he do with the field?" He usually plants the field in rye, she explained; why, only the other day he drove up with a wagon carrying a plough, one of his sons was with him, they left the wagon at the gate, the two of them unloaded the plough, they hitched the—but the boy interrupted severely: "Does the field go all the way over to the brook?" The conversation continued in this vein, always at cross-purposes, and growing increasingly humorous to eavesdroppers as its formal principle was inexorably continued. Note in *Salome,* however, this mechanism serving to produce a very different effect:

"SALOME: *(to Iokanaan)* . . . Suffer me to kiss thy mouth.

"IOKANAAN: Never! daughter of Babylon! Daughter of Sodom! Never!

"SALOME: I will kiss thy mouth, Iokanaan. . . .

"THE YOUNG SYRIAN: . . . Look not at this man, look not at him. I cannot endure it. . . . Princess, do not speak these things.

"SALOME: I will kiss thy mouth, Iokanaan."

And as the Young Syrian, in despair, slays himself and falls dead at her feet, she continues: "Suffer me to kiss thy mouth, Iokanaan."

Turning now to Wordsworth's "We Are Seven":

> " 'You say that two at Conway dwell,
>   And two are gone to sea,
>   Yet ye are seven. I pray you tell,
>   Sweet maid, how this may be.'

> "Then did the little Maid reply,
>   'Seven boys and girls are we;
>   Two of us in the churchyard lie,
>   Beneath the churchyard tree.' "

The poet argues with her: there were seven in all, two are now dead—so it follows that there are only five. But when he has made his point,

> " 'How many are you, then,' said I,
>   'If they two are in heaven?'
>   Quick was the little Maid's reply,
>   'O Master! we are seven.' "

Humor, *sournoiserie,* sentiment—we may now turn to Racine, where we find this talking at cross-purposes employed to produce a very poignant tragic irony. Agamemnon has secretly arranged to sacrifice his daughter, Iphigenia, on the altar; he is telling her so, but haltingly and cryptically, confessing and concealing at once; she does not grasp the meaning of his words but feels their ominousness. She has heard, she says, that Calchas is planning a sacrifice to appease the gods. Agamemnon exclaims: Would that he could turn these gods from their outrageous demands (his words referring to the oracle which requires her death, as the audience knows, but Iphigenia does not). Will the offering take place soon? she asks.—Sooner than Agamemnon wishes.—Will

she be allowed to be present?—Alas! says Agamemnon.—
You say no more, says Iphigenia.—"You will be there, my
daughter"—the conflict in meanings being heightened by
the fact that each of Agamemnon's non sequitur rejoinders
rhymes with Iphigenia's question:

"IPHIGÉNIE: *Périsse le Troyen auteur de nos alarmes!*

AGAMEMNON: *Sa perte à ses vainqueurs coûtera bien des larmes.*

IPHIGÉNIE: *Les dieux deignent surtout prendre soin de vos jours!*

AGAMEMNON: *Les dieux depuis un temps me sont cruels et sourds.*

IPHIGÉNIE: *Calchas, dit-on, prépare un pompeux sacrifice?*

AGAMEMNON: *Puissé-je auparavant fléchir leur injustice!*

IPHIGÉNIE: *L'offrira-t-on bientôt?*

AGAMEMNON: *Plus tôt que je ne veux.*

IPHIGÉNIE: *Me sera-t-il permis de me joindre à vos veux?*
           Verra-t-on à l'autel votre heureuse famille?

AGAMEMNON: *Hélas!*

IPHIGÉNIE: *Vous vous taisez!*

AGAMEMNON: *Vous y serez, ma fille."*

Perhaps the line, "Hurry up please, it's time," in the public
house scene of *The Waste Land,* as it is repeated and un-
answered, could illustrate the use of this formal contrivance
for still another effect.

THE INDIVIDUATION OF FORMS

11. *Appeal of Forms.* Form, having to do with the creation and gratification of needs, is "correct" in so far as it gratifies the needs which it creates. The appeal of the form in
this sense is obvious: form *is* the appeal. The appeal of pro-

gressive and repetitive forms as they figure in the major organization of a work, needs no further explanation. Conventional form is a shiftier topic, particularly since the conventional forms demanded by one age are as resolutely shunned by another. Often they owe their presence in art to a survival from a different situation (as the invocation to the Muses is the conventionalization of a prayer based upon an earlier belief in the divine inspiration of poetry; and the chorus in the religious rites of Dionysus survives in the secular drama that grew out of these rites). At other times a conventional form may arise from a definite functional purpose, as the ebb, flow, and close of a sonnet became a conventional form through repeated usage. Thereafter a reader will be disturbed at a sonnet of fifteen lines, even though it attain precisely the ebb, flow, and close that distinguishes the sonnet. The reader has certain categorical expectations which the poet must meet. As for the formality of beginnings and endings—such procedures as the greeting of the New Year, the ceremony at laying a cornerstone, the "house-warming," the funeral, all indicate that the human mind is prone to feel beginnings and endings *as such.*

When we turn to minor form and carry examination down to the individual sentence, or the individual figure of speech, the relation between form and the gratification of desire becomes admittedly more tenuous. The formal appeal of the single sentence need not, it is true, be sought in the sentence alone—the sentence can also "gratify" us by its place in a context (it contributes to progressive form in so far as it contains a statement that advances the plot; and it contributes to repetitive form if, for instance, it corroborates our expectations with respect to a certain character). But, since the single sentence has form, we are forced by our thesis to consider the element of gratification in the sentence apart from its context. There are certain rudimentary kinds of balance in which the factor of desire is perceptible, as when a succession of monosyllables arouses the "need" of a polysyllabic word to break their monotony. And the same factor exists clearly enough in the periodic sentence, where the withholding of some important detail until the last drives us forward to the close. But is not every sentence a "periodic" sentence? If one, for instance, enters a room and says simply, "The man . . ." unless the auditor knows enough about the man to finish the sentence in his own thoughts, his spontaneous rejoinder will be, "The man what?" A naming must be completed by a doing, either explicit or implicit. The subject demands a predicate as resolutely as the antecedent of a musical phrase in Mozart calls for its consequent. Admittedly, when we carry the discussion to so small a particle (almost like discussing one brush stroke as a test of a definition of form in painting) the element of "gratification" will not usually be prominent. The formal satisfaction of completion will be clear only in cases where the process of completing is stressed, as in the periodic sentence. Otherwise it can be better revealed by our dissatisfaction with an uncompleted thought than by our satisfaction with a completed one.

The appeal of form as exemplified in rhythm enjoys a special advantage in that rhythm is more closely allied with "bodily" processes. Systole and diastole, alternation of the feet in walking, inhalation and exhalation, up and down, in and out, back and forth, such are the types of distinctly motor experiences "tapped" by rhythm. Rhythm is so natural to the organism that even a succession of uniform beats will be interpreted as a succession of accented and unaccented beats. The rhythm of a page, in setting up a corresponding rhythm in the body, creates marked degrees of expectancy, or acquiescence. A rhythm is a promise which the poet makes to the reader—and in proportion as the reader comes to rely upon this promise, he falls into a state of general surrender which makes him more likely to accept without resistance the rest of the poet's material. In becoming receptive to so much, he becomes receptive to still more. The varied rhythms of prose also have their "motor" analogies. A reader sensitive to prose rhythms is like a man hurrying through a crowd; at one time he must halt, at another time he can leap forward; he darts perilously between saunterers; he guards himself in turning sharp corners. We mean that in all rhythmic experiences one's "muscular imagination" is touched. Similarly with sounds, there is some analogy to actual movement, since sounds may rise and fall, and in a remote way one rises and falls with them.

12. *"Priority" of forms.* There are formal patterns which distinguish our experience. They apply in art, since they apply outside of art. The accelerated motion of a falling body, the cycle of a storm, the gradations of a sunrise, the stages of a cholera epidemic, the ripening of crops—in all such instances we find the material of progressive form. Repetitive form applies to all manner of orientation, for we can continue to discuss a subject only by taking up in turn various aspects of it. (Recalling the schoolmen's subdivisions of a topic: *quis, quid, ubi, quibus auxiliis, cur, quo modo, quando.* One talks about a thing by talking about something else.) We establish a direction by co-ordinates; we establish a curve by three points, and thereupon can so place other points that they will be intercepted by this curve. Thus, though forms need not be prior to experience, they are certainly prior to the work of art exemplifying them. Psychology and philosophy may decide whether they are innate or resultant; so far as the work of art is concerned they simply *are*: when one turns to the production or enjoyment of a work of art, a formal equipment is already present, and the

effects of art are involved in its utilization. Such ultimate minor forms as contrast, comparison, metaphor, series, bathos, chiasmus, are based upon our modes of understanding anything; they are implicit in the processes of abstraction and generalization by which we think. (When analyzed so closely, they manifest the principles of repetitive and progressive form so frailly that we might better speak of coexistent unity and diversity—"something" in relation to "something else"—which is probably the basic distinction of our earliest perceptions. The most rudimentary manifestation of such coexistent unity and diversity in art is perhaps observable in two rhyming monosyllables, room—doom, where diversity of sound in the initial consonants coexists with unity of sound in the vowels and final consonants, a relation describable either as repetitive or as progressive.)

Such basic forms may, for all that concerns us, be wholly conventional. The subject–predicate form of sentence, for instance, has sanction enough if we have learned to expect it. It may be "natural" only as a path worn across a field is natural. But if experience has worn a path, the path is there —and in using the path we are obeying the authority of a prior form.

An ability to function in a certain way implies gratification in so functioning. A capacity is not something which lies dormant until used—a capacity is a command to act in a certain way. Thus a pinioned bird, though it has learned that flight is impossible, must yet spread out its wings and go through the motions of flying: its muscles, being equipped for flight, require the process. Similarly, if a dog lacks a bone, he will gnaw at a block of wood; not that he is hungry —for he may have his fill of meat—but his teeth, in their fitness to endure the strain of gnawing, feel the need of enduring that strain. So the formal aspects of art appeal in that they exercise formal potentialities of the reader. They enable the mind to follow processes amenable to it. Mother Goose is little more than an exerciser of simple mental functions. It is almost wholly formal, with processes of comparing, contrasting, and arranging. Though the jingles may, in some instance, have originated as political lampoons, etc., the ideas as adapted in the nursery serve purely as gymnastics in the fundamental processes of form.

The forms of art, to summarize, are not exclusively "æsthetic." They can be said to have a prior existence in the experiences of the person hearing or reading the work of art. They parallel processes which characterize his experiences outside of art.

13. *Individuation of forms.* Since there are no forms of art which are not forms of experience outside of art, we may —so far as form is concerned—discuss the single poem or drama as an individuation of formal principles. Each work re-embodies the formal principles in different subject-matter. A "metaphor" is a concept, an abstraction—but a specific metaphor, exemplified by specific images, is an "individuation." Its appeal as form resides in the fact that its particular subject-matter enables the mind to follow a metaphor-process. In this sense we would restore the Platonic relationship between form and matter. A form is a way of experiencing; and such a form is made available in art when, by the use of specific subject-matter, it enables us to experience in this way. The images of art change greatly with changes in the environment and the ethical systems out of which they arise; but the principles of art, as individuated in these changing images, will be found to recur in all art, where they are individuated in one subject-matter or another. Accordingly, the concept of the individuation of forms constitutes the bridge by which we move from a consideration of form to a consideration of subject-matter.

14. *Form and information*. The necessity of embodying form in subject-matter gives rise to certain "diseases" of form. The subject-matter tends to take on an intrinsic interest, to appeal independently of its functional uses. Thus, whereas realism originated to meet formal requirements (the introduction of life-like details to make outlandish plots plausible), it became an end in itself; whereas it arose in the attempt to make the unreal realistic, it ended by becoming a purpose in itself and making the real realistic. Similarly, description grows in assertiveness until novelists write descriptions, not for their use in the arousing and fulfilling of expectation, but because the novelists have something to describe which they consider interesting in itself (a volcano, a remarkable savage tribe, an unusual thicket). This tendency becomes frankly "scientific" in the thesis drama and the psychological novel, where the matter is offered for its value as the "exposure" of a burning issue. In the psychological novel, the reader may often follow the hero's mental processes as noteworthy facts, just as he would follow them in a scientific treatise on the human mind, except that in the novel the facts are less schematically arranged from the standpoint of scientific presentation. In so far as the details in a work are offered, not for their bearing upon the business of molding and meeting the reader's expectations, but because these details are interesting in themselves, the appeal of form retreats behind the appeal of information. Atrophy of form follows hypertrophy of information.

There is, obviously, no "right" proportion of the two. A novelist, for instance, must give enough description for us to feel the conviction of his story's background. Description, to this extent, is necessary in the interests of form—and there is no clearly distinguishable point at which description for the purposes of the plot goes over into description for its own sake. Similarly, a certain amount of psychological data con-

Has earlier said that he wants to restore info. to it rightful place as minor (p. 34)

cerning the characters of a fiction helps the author to make
the characters of moment to the reader, and thus has a formal function in the affecting of the reader's desires: yet the
psychology can begin to make claims of its own, and at
times the writer will analyze his hero not because analysis
is formally needed at this point, but because the writer has
some disclosures which he considers interesting in themselves.

The hypertrophy of information likewise tends to interfere
with our enjoyment in the repetition of a work. For the presence of information as a factor in literature has enabled
writers to rely greatly upon ignorance as a factor in appeal.
Thus, they will relieve the reader's ignorance about a certain
mountain of Tibet, but when they have done so they will
have less to "tell" him at a second reading. Surprise and suspense are the major devices for the utilization of ignorance
(the psychology of information), for when they are depended
upon, the reader's interest in the work is based primarily
upon his ignorance of its outcome. In the classic drama,
where the psychology of form is emphasized, we have not
surprise but disclosure (the surprise being a surprise not to
the audience, but to the characters); and likewise suspense
here is not based upon our ignorance of the forthcoming
scenes. There is, perhaps, more formal suspense at a second
reading than at a first in a scene such as Hamlet's giving of
the pipes to Guildenstern. It is the suspense of certain forces
gathering to produce a certain result. It is the suspense of a
rubber band which we see being tautened. We know that it
will be snapped—there is thus no ignorance of the outcome;
our satisfaction arises from our participation in the process, ✶ _(collaboration)_
from the fact that the beginnings of the dialogue lead us
to feel the logic of its close.

Painting, architecture, music are probably more amenable
to repetition without loss because the formal aspects are not
so obscured by the subject-matter in which they are em-

bodied. One can repeat with pleasure a jingle from Mother Goose, where the formality is obvious, yet one may have no interest whatsoever in memorizing a psychological analysis in a fiction. He may wish to remember the observations themselves, but his own words are as serviceable as the author's. And if he does choose to memorize the particular wording of the author, and recites it with pleasure, the passage will be found to have a formal, as well as an informational, validity.

15. *Form and Ideology.* The artist's manipulations of the reader's desires involve his use of what the reader considers desirable. If the reader believes in monogamistic marriage, and in the code of fidelity surrounding it, the poet can exploit this belief in writing an *Othello.* But the form of his drama is implicated in the reader's belief, and Othello's conduct would hardly seem "syllogistic" in polyandrous Tibet. Similarly, the conventional form which marks the close of Baudelaire's *Femmes Damnées,* as he turns from the dialogue of the two Lesbians to his eloquent apostrophe, *"Descendez, descendez, lamentables victimes,"* is an effect built out of precisely that intermingling of church morality and profanation which Baudelaire always relies upon for his deepest effects. He writes for neither pure believers nor pure infidels, but for infidels whose infidelity greatly involves the surviving vocabulary of belief. In war times, the playwright who would depict a villain has only to designate his man as a foreign spy—at other times he must be more inventive to find something so exploitable in the ideology of his audience. A slight change in ideology, in fact, can totally reverse our judgments as to the form which it embodies. Thus, Euripides was accused of misusing the *deus ex machina.* In his *Iphigenia at Aulis,* for instance, his syllogistic progression leads the heroine inexorably to the sacrificial altar—whereupon a

god descends and snatches her unharmed from her father's knife. Approached from the ideology of an Aristotle, this would constitute a violation of form, since the dramatic causality leads to one end and the poet gives us another. But we can consider the matter differently: the drama was a survival of a religious rite; as such, the god certainly had a place in it; Euripides frankly attempted to regain some of the earlier dramatic forms which Æschylus and Sophocles had suppressed and which brought out more clearly its religious affiliations; could we not, accordingly, look upon the appearance of the god as a part of Euripides' program? Euripides would, that is, write a play in which the details of the plot led the heroine so inexorably towards destruction that nothing could save her but the intervention of the gods. By this ideology, the closing theophany is formally correct: it is not a way of avoiding a bad ending (the "syllogistically" required death of an Iphigenia who has won the audience's sympathies); it is a syllogistic preparation for the god's appearance. As another instance of how the correctness of the form depends upon the ideology, we may consider a piece of juvenile fiction for Catholic boys. The hero will be consistently a hero: he will show bravery, honesty, kindness to the oppressed, strength in sports, gentleness to women—in every way, by the tenets of repetitive form, he will repeat the fact that he is a hero. And among these repetitions will be his converting of Indians to Catholicism. To a Catholic boy, this will be one more repetition of his identity as an ideal hero; but to the Protestant boy, approaching the work from a slightly different ideology, repetitive form will be endangered at this point.

The shifts in ideology being continuous, not only from age to age but from person to person, the individuation of universal forms through specific subject-matter can bring the formal principles themselves into jeopardy.

16. *Re-individuation of forms*. The best proof that there is "individuation of forms" is the fact that there is "re-individuation of forms." The simplest instance is the literal translation, which fills the form with a complete change of matter (the words out of one social context are replaced by parallel words out of another social context). In free translation, the correspondences are conceived more broadly, the re-individuation often being effected not only by vocabulary, but also by adjustments to differences in ideology. Thus, a translator was bewildered by a chapter in German which spoke continually of the hero's spirit, or soul, or mind (*Geist*); the author told at great length what the hero's *Geist* was doing, wanting to do, and wanting not to do; but there seemed no natural equivalent for this in English until the translator discovered that, everywhere the German said "his soul desired such-and-such," the English could say quite simply "he desired such-and-such." In Germany the ideology behind the Hegelian vocabulary still flourishes in some quarters, thus making this survival of *Geist* in such a usage much less an oddity than it would be in America—wherefore the translator's "free re-individuation" took this slight difference of ideology into account. . . . It is with the adaptation of plays that the re-individuating process usually goes farthest in altering to fit differences of ideology. The "play doctors" think nothing of so re-individuating a German war play for American consumption that friend and foe of the original are reversed in the adaptation. Or one might, for contemporary theatrical uses, best "re-individuate" an ancient burlesque of political conditions in Athens by putting the Mayor of New York in place of Pericles. Playwrights are the arch-reindividuators. The writers of revues make a definite practice of adapting the vulgar story of the smoker, so re-individuating its underlying form by a more temperate situation and plot that the story becomes available for produc-

tion on the stage, thus translating a story conceived by "private life" ideology into a story suited to "public life" ideology. (Since in Japan it is customary to smile on mentioning the death of a close friend, were we completely re-individuating a Japanese mention of smiling under such conditions, we might say, not "he smiled," but "his face fell," as the Western equivalent. We should thus be translating the accepted social usage of Japan into the corresponding accepted social usage of the West.)

Perhaps the most elaborate re-individuation in all history is James Joyce's *Ulysses*. But whereas in most instances the purpose of the new individuations is to make changes which reproduce under one set of conditions an effect originally obtained under another set of conditions, in the case of *Ulysses* each individuation is given a strictly "un-Homeric" equivalent. The new individuations intentionally alter the effect. The *Ulysses* is the Anti-Odyssey.

PATTERNS OF EXPERIENCE

17. *Universal experiences.* The various kinds of moods, feelings, emotions, perceptions, sensations, and attitudes discussed in the manuals of psychology and exemplified in works of art, we consider universal experiences. Mockery, despair, grimness, *sang-froid,* wonder, lamentation, melancholy, hatred, hopefulness, bashfulness, relief, boredom, dislike—for our present purposes it does not matter how these are grouped, which are "basic" and which derivative, how many or how few there are said to be: we call them universal because all men, under certain conditions, and when not in mental or physical collapse, are capable of experiencing them. Nor does it matter whether we choose to call them mental or somatic; it is sufficient that they arise. They could equally well be discussed as processes; for convenience' sake we discuss them as states.

18. *Modes of experience*. The universal experiences are implicated in specific modes of experience: they arise out of a relationship between the organism and its environment. Frustration and gratification of bodily needs; ethical systems; customs; the whole ideology or code of values among which one is raised—these are involved in the modes of experience. A newborn child manifests fear at loss of physical support; but an adult may experience loss of support with pleasure, as in diving, while greatly fearing the loss of support which would be involved in his alienating the good opinion of his neighbors. At restriction of movement the infant manifests rage; and a man who might without rage endure the binding of his arms for hours would flare up in two minutes at an attempt to confine him in an argument. Grief at deprivation is universal—yet grief at deprivation may be exemplified in lovers' partings, financial ruin, or subtle loss of self-esteem. The range of universal experiences may be lived on a mountain top, at sea, among a primitive tribe, in a salon—the modes of experience so differing in each instance that people in two different schemes of living can derive very different universal experiences from an identical event. The hypochondriac facing a soiled glove may experience a deep fear of death to which the trained soldier facing a cannon is insensitive.

The same universal experience could invariably accompany the same mode of experience only if all men's modes of experience were identical.

19. *Patterns of experience*. Experience arising out of a relationship between an organism and its environment, the adjustments of the organism will depend upon the nature of the environment. By "adjustments of the organism" we refer to any kind of adaptation; thus: firm musculature as the concomitant of life under pioneer conditions; obesity as

See pg. 172 for clarification about difference between modes & patterns, the concomitant of plenty and confinement; vindictiveness as the concomitant of oppression; timidity as the concomitant of protection; trustfulness as the concomitant of fair dealing—a distinction in the environment calling forth a distinction in the organism. An "adjustment" need not be a "good adjustment." It is as much an "adjustment," in our sense, for the organism to die of a bullet as for the organism to dodge one. It is equally an adjustment to avoid a calamity, to remove the cause of a calamity, or to become so "closed" by philosophy or hysteria that the calamity is unfelt. We do not mean that a given distinction of the environment always calls forth the same distinction of the organism. A condition of plenty and confinement may lead, for instance, not to obesity but to a régime of diet and calisthenics. Protection may lead, not to timidity, but to the protected person's determination to put himself upon his own resources. We refer simply to the fact that the adjusting organism will take some particular environmental condition into account. A particular environmental condition may be: a cruel father, an indulgent mother, a long stretch of poverty, the death of a favorite aunt, rough treatment at the hands of other boys, gentle years in a garden, what you will. Any such specific environmental condition calls forth and stresses certain of the universal experiences as being more relevant to it, with a slighting of those less relevant. Such selections are "patterns of experience." They distinguish us as "characters." The protest of a Byron, the passive resistance of a Gandhi, the hopefulness of a Browning, the satirical torment of a Swift, the primness of a Jane Austen—these are all patterns of experience.

We do not imply that these patterns are wholly the result of environment. They result from the combination of organism and environment—and organisms presumably differ as much as environments. A more sensitive organism, for instance, might need a less emphatic environmental condition to cause it pain—indeed, too emphatic an environmental condition might cause it, not pain, but a compensatory blunting of pain. A direct and simple personality may arise when the environment reinforces the best aptitudes of the organism. A complex, hesitant personality may arise when the process of "learning," or adjustment to the environment, entailed the slighting of the organism's best aptitudes and the forcible development of lesser ones. However, the essential fact for our discussion is not the genesis of the patterns, but their existence.

Once they exist, though they may be in themselves results, they become in turn "creative." The method of adjustment (the particular selection of universal experiences) which the organism has developed to face specific environmental conditions is subsequently applied to other environmental conditions. A man who has been betrayed in a matter of vast importance to him may henceforth distrust people deserving of his full confidence. Such selectiveness may be a temporary pattern, or it may influence his judgments and social relationships for the remainder of his life. Whether the pattern is permanent (as a lasting state of distrust) or temporary (as a sudden state of grief following a loss), while it endures it tends to make over the world in its own image. Jealousy is a "creative" or "interpretive" principle, enabling the jealous man to find startling grounds for jealousy where less jealous persons would note nothing at all. Thus, arising presumably as a method of adjustment to one condition, the pattern may become a method of meeting other conditions —may become a typical manner of experiencing.

20. *The Symbol.* The Symbol is the verbal parallel to a pattern of experience. The poet, for instance, may pity himself for his undeserved neglect, and this self-pity may color

his day. It may be so forceful, and so frequently recurrent as to become selective, so that he finds ever new instances of his unappreciated worth. Self-pity assumes enough prominence in his case to become a pattern of experience. If he converts his pattern into a plot, "The King and the Peasant" (about a King who has but the trappings of kingliness and a Peasant who is, in the true sense, a King) he has produced a Symbol. He might have chosen other Symbols to verbalize the same pattern. In fact, if his pattern continues to obsess him, he undoubtedly will exemplify the same pattern in other Symbols: he will next produce "The Man Against the Mob," or "A Saint Dying in Neglect." Or he may be still more devious, and finding his own problems writ large in the life of some historic figure, he may give us a vigorous biography of the Little Corporal.

The Symbol is often quite obvious, as in *Childe Harold, Madame Bovary, Euphues, Don Quixote, Tom Sawyer, Wilhelm Meister, Hamlet.* In lyrics of mood it is not so readily summed up in a name. It is pervasive but not condensed. The Symbol of *The Tempest?* Perhaps it is more nearly condensed in the songs and doings of Ariel than elsewhere in the play, but essentially it is a complex attitude which pervades the setting, plot, and characters. The Symbol might be called a word invented by the artist to specify a particular grouping or pattern or emphasizing of experiences—and the work of art in which the Symbol figures might be called a definition of this word. The novel, *Madame Bovary,* is an elaborate definition of a new word in our vocabulary. In the lyric, in *The Tempest,* the Symbol is present as definition, though not as a word. The Symbol is a formula.

21. *Appeal of the Symbol.* The Symbol is perhaps most overwhelming in its effect when the artist's and the reader's patterns of experience closely coincide. *Childe Harold,* the

Symbol for Byron's patterns of experience, becomes thus the word or formula which mute Byrons, with the same patterns, were awaiting. The Symbol may also serve to force patterns upon the audience, however, the universal experiences being capable of other groupings or patterns than those which characterize the particular reader; thus: As people in fright (artist's pattern) cry out (Symbol), so an outcry (same Symbol) will be most terrifying to those already tense with fright (audience's pattern same as artist's pattern)—but the outcry (same Symbol) may also frighten those who were at rest (audience with different pattern, but susceptible to the authority of the Symbol).

A Symbol appeals:

As the interpretation of a situation. It can, by its function as name and definition, give simplicity and order to an otherwise unclarified complexity. It provides a terminology of thoughts, actions, emotions, attitudes, for codifying a pattern of experience. The artist, through experiencing intensively or extensively a certain pattern, becomes as it were an expert, a specialist, in this pattern. And his skill in articulation is expended upon the schematizing of his subject. The schematizing is done not by abstraction, as in science, but by idealization, by presenting in a "pure" or consistent manner some situation which, as it appears among the contingencies of real life, is less effectively co-ordinated; the idealization is the elimination of irrelevancies.

By favoring the acceptance of a situation. At times the situation revealed by the Symbol may not be particularly complex, but our minds have been closed to the situation through the exigencies of practical life. The Symbol can enable us to admit, for instance, the existence of a certain danger which we had emotionally denied. A humorous Symbol enables us to admit the situation by belittling it; a satirical Symbol enables us to admit the situation by permitting us to feel aloof from it; a tragic Symbol enables us to admit the situation by making us feel the dignity of being in such a situation; the comic Symbol enables us to admit the situation by making us feel our power to surmount it. A Symbol may also force us to admit a situation by the sheer thoroughness of the Symbol, but if the situation is one which we had strong motives for denying, and if the Symbol is not presented by some such accompanying attitude as above noted, the admitting of the situation will probably be accompanied by a revulsion against the Symbol.

As the corrective of a situation. Life in the city arouses a compensatory interest in life on a farm, with the result that Symbols of farm life become appealing; or a dull life in the city arouses a compensatory interest in Symbols depicting a brilliant life in the city; etc. In such cases the actual situation to which the Symbol is adapted is left unformulated. Most stories of romantic love are probably in this class.

As the exerciser of "submerged" experience. A capacity to function in a certain way (as we have pointed out in the discussion of form) is not merely something which lies on a shelf until used—a capacity to function in a certain way is an obligation so to function. Even those "universal experiences" which the reader's particular patterns of experience happen to slight are in a sense "candidates"—they await with some aggression their chance of being brought into play. Thus though the artist's pattern may be different from the reader's, the Symbol by touching on submerged patterns in the reader may "stir remote depths." Symbols of cruelty, horror, and incest may often owe their appeal to such causes.

As an "emancipator." (The explosive success of "scarlet-sister" literature, for instance, as *La Dame aux Camélias.*) The situation in which the reader happens to be placed requires of him an adjustment which certain of his moral values prohibit (in this case, sexual inclinations discountenanced by the Church). The Symbol, by appealing to certain other of his moral values (in this case, the respect for heroines possessing "deep humanity," "fine womanly qualities") may make the attitude "morally" acceptable. Here certain moral assumptions are pitted against others, with the reader's "need" on the side of the attacking assumptions. (Assumptions of what is admirable, that is, are pitted against assumptions of what is contemnable, with the reader's desire for greater laxity serving to weight the assumptions of what is admirable. Accordingly, if some kind of conduct is, by our code of values, called wicked, absurd, low-caste, wasteful, etc., and if the situation in which we are placed requires this reprehensible kind of conduct, that Symbol will be effective which, by manipulating other values in our code, makes such conduct seem virtuous, discerning, refined, accurate, etc. The appeal of the Symbol as "emancipator" involves fundamentally a mere shifting of terms in this way: leisure for indolence, foolhardiness for bravery, thrift for miserliness, improvidence for generosity, et cetera or vice versa.

As a vehicle for "artistic" effects. A Malvolio, a Falstaff, a Coriolanus. To a degree their appeal is in their sheer value as inventions. They are a nimble running of scales; they display the poet's farthest reaches of virtuosity. The love of the impromptu—the feeling that brilliance is being given out with profusion and overwhelming spontaneity. Inasmuch as everybody yearns to say one brilliant thing, perhaps this appeal of the Symbol is most poignant of all. At least, it claims a major rôle in the smart repartee of the American theatre.

This discussion of Symbolic appeal is not offered as exhaustive, but as illustrative. Nor are the means of appeal mutually exclusive. Essentially, we might summarize the entire list by saying that the Symbol appeals either as the orienting of a situation, or as the adjustment to a situation, or as both.

22. *The Symbol as Generating Principle.* When the poet has converted his pattern of experience into a Symbolic equivalent, the Symbol becomes a guiding principle in itself. Thus, once our poet suffering self-pity has hit upon the plot of "The King and the Peasant," he finds himself with many problems remote from his self-pity. Besides showing his King as a weakling, he must show him as a King—whereupon accounts of court life. Similarly the treatment of the Peasant will entail harvest scenes, dances, descriptions of the Peasant's hut. There will be the Peasant's Wife and the Queen and a host of subsidiary characters. As the Symbol is ramified, Symbols within Symbols will arise, many of these secondary Symbols with no direct bearing upon the pattern of experience behind the key Symbol. These secondary or ramifying Symbols can be said to bear upon the underlying pattern of experience only in so far as they contribute to the workings of the key Symbol.

Again: Symbols will be subtilized in ways not contributory to the pattern. The weak King cannot be too weak, the manly Peasant cannot be too manly—thus we find the Poet "defending" to an extent the very character whom he would denigrate, and detracting from the character who is to triumph. Such considerations arise with the adoption of the Symbol, which is the conversion of an experiential pattern into a formula for affecting an audience.

The Symbol, in other words, brings up problems extrinsic to the pattern of experience behind it. The underlying pattern, that is, remains the same whether the poet writes "The King and the Peasant," "The Man Against the Mob," or "A Saint Dying in Neglect." But in each case the Symbol is a generating principle which entails a selection of different subtilizations and ramifications. Thus, the difference between the selectivity of a dream and the selectivity of art is that the dream obeys no principle of selection but the underlying pattern, whereas art, which expands by the ramifying of the Symbol, has the Symbol as a principle of selection.

23. *Ramifications of the Symbol.* A theoretically perfect Symbol would, in all its ramifications, reveal the underlying pattern of experience. It is only in cases of mental derangement, however, that a wholly consistent and unchangeable pattern is observable in such minute particles as the single word. One shell-shocked patient might fall into spasms of terror at the sound of an "s," since it suggests to him the sizzling fuse of a bomb. But the normal man's patterns are never so intense as this; and in proportion as they widen, the "neutral" zone of specific words also widens. To one who has just lost a child, even an author's very humorous reference to children may bring tears; so long as the loss is poignant, the word that suggests the loss ("symbolizes" the loss) touches a pronounced pattern of experience in the reader. Ordinarily, however, the reader is less imperious: under normal conditions, mention of children will not symbolize the loss of a child unless the author has so arranged his page as to aim at this particular Symbolization. Otherwise, the author can exploit one of several mutually antagonistic experiences of the reader: the reader is free to follow him, for instance, whether he chooses to depict children as angels or to depict them as an unending annoyance. Words generally have little more than a denotative function—they point to something. And when they point to something about which we have no great emotional concern, they necessarily fail to reveal any marked underlying pattern.

A word usually encompasses a considerable range of "neutral" experiences—experiences, that is, which bear upon the denotative rather than the affective aspects of the object which it names. A hammer (and thus by transference the word "hammer") may be a strong affective image to a man once threatened with a hammer under unforgettable circumstances—and when he uses the word the bias of his experiences may conceivably be revealed by the contiguity of another ominous image—but to all men a hammer is an implement for driving nails, and in this connection the word is "neutral," purely "denotative." The affective shades, of course, differ with the individual reader, and can normally be either fostered or canceled by the designs of the artist.

The underlying pattern is observable when an apparently arbitrary or illogical association of ideas can be shown to possess an "emotional" connective. The logical laxity of imagism has enabled psychologists, for instance, to discover such emotional connectives in the work of Verhaeren, connectives distinctly arising from the pattern of experience underlying his work. Similarly, the examination of concordances can reveal "patterns" to a degree. On going through all the lines of a poet in which a certain word appears, the reader can often note a common quality distinguishing the lot. Observe in Shakespeare, for instance, the many passages in which the word "hour" appears with ominous connotations. Note by its contexts the strong distrust which seems to surround the word "future" (a vague danger to be prepared for) in contrast with the general confidence of the passages in which this word appears in Browning. Consider the notions of power and energy surrounding the word "demon" in Keats, whereas the word is quite innocuous in Tennyson.

The underlying pattern is best observable when words refer to no specific thing—as "liberty, equality, fraternity"— "my country"—"the good of society." In such cases, the contexts in which the words appear will generally be constants. (Though, be it noted: if a patriot were depicting a villain, he might have the villain say "my country" slurringly. This would be the equivalent to the patriot's saying "my country" devoutly. We should thus feel justified in considering such opposites as further evidence of a constant.)

24. *Complexity and Power.* The Symbol tends towards the two extremes of power and complexity. A Symbol is "powerful" in proportion as it limits its ramifications to a strict reinforcement of the poet's underlying pattern (as in the unified effect of a story by Poe, or in a poem such as Keats's "Ode to a Nightingale"). A Symbol is "complex" in proportion as its ramifications follow the "logic" of the Symbol rather than the emotions of the underlying pattern. The author of "The King and the Peasant" produces a complex Symbol in so far as he submerges his self-pity beneath a panorama of court life, peasant customs, comic relief, subtilizations, subsidiary Symbols (so that the underlying pattern which originally gave rise to the Symbol will be revealed only at "pivotal points," such as the final triumphing of the Peasant).

The peril of complexity is diffusion. The peril of power is monotony.

As an instance of a "complex" Symbol in miniature let us quote from Darwin:

"From experiments which I have lately tried, I have found that the visits of bees are necessary for the fertilization of some kinds of clover; the humble-bees alone visit red clover (*Trifolium pratense*), as other bees cannot reach the nectar. Hence I have very little doubt, that if the whole genus of humble-bees became extinct or very rare in England, the heartsease and red clover would become very rare or wholly disappear. The number of humble-bees in any district depends in a great degree on the number of field mice, which destroy their combs and nests; and Mr. H. Newman, who has long attended to the habits of humble-bees, believes that 'more than two-thirds of them are thus destroyed all over

England." Now the number of mice is largely dependent, as everyone knows, on the number of cats; and Mr. Newman says, 'near villages and small towns I have found the nests of humble-bees more numerous than elsewhere, which I attribute to the number of cats that destroy the mice.' Hence, it is quite credible that the presence of a feline animal in large numbers in a district might determine, through the intervention, first of mice, and then of bees, the frequency of certain flowers in that district."

And the same pattern, as a Symbol of "power," would be found in "The House That Jack Built."

RITUAL

25. *Ideology.* Expanding our earlier discussion of ideology: If people believe something, the poet can use this belief to get an effect. If they despise treachery, for instance, he can awaken their detestation by the portrait of a traitor. If they admire self-sacrifice, he can set them to admiring by a tragedy of self-sacrifice. If they hold the earth the center of the universe, he can base the dignity of man upon geocentricity. By an ideology is meant the nodus of beliefs and judgments which the artist can exploit for his effects. It varies from one person to another, and from one age to another—but in so far as its general acceptance and its stability are more stressed than its particular variations from person to person and from age to age, an ideology is a "culture." If an entire nation feels abhorrence at the profaning of a certain kind of altar, and agrees as to how the altar could be profaned, to that extent it possesses a "culture." But there are cultures within cultures, since a society can be subdivided into groups with divergent standards and interests. Each of these subdivisions of a culture may possess its own characteristic ideology (contrast the ideology of a young radical in the coal mines with the ideol-

ogy of a retired banker touring the Mediterranean), but in so far as they overlap they belong to the same culture (both the radical and the banker, for instance, may despise an informer). Generally, the ideology of an individual is a slight variant of the ideology distinguishing the class among which he arose.

The artist obtains his effects by manipulating our ideological assumptions in many ways. The simplest is "idealization," as when a Symbol so thoroughly exemplifies the pitiable that we can be thoroughly aroused to pity. In general, his effects are obtained by the playing of some assumptions against others (the author of "The King and the Peasant," who would show that real kingliness can be found in peasants, and kings can be boors, does this by pitting the assumptions of spiritual distinction against the assumptions of social distinction). Tragedy is based upon the firm acceptance of an ideology (an author can most ably arouse our grief over the death of a hero when he and we are in complete agreement as to what qualities are heroic). For this reason perhaps the humorous writers are better equipped today than the tragic ones, since humor results from a discrepancy between ideological assumptions, and the great conflict of standards in contemporary society gives the artist a considerable range of such discrepancies to select from. Thus when Will Rogers, in commenting on the presence of U.S. Marines in Nicaragua, said: "All this trouble about Nicaragua—why don't they come out and fight us like a man?" he was, in so dealing with the discrepancy between the power of the United States and the power of the "enemy," attaining humor by pitting the assumptions of sportsmanship (we should choose an opponent our size) against the assumptions of patriotism (our country always in the right).

Many of the beliefs exploited by poetry in the past were backed by the authority of the Church; in the future, beliefs may be to a great extent founded upon science. There is perhaps no essential difference between religious and scientific "foundations," however, as religion is probably the outgrowth of magic, itself a "science" based on theories of causation which were subsequently modified or discredited. Magic, religion, and science are alike in that they foster a body of thought concerning the nature of the universe and man's relation to it. All three offer possibilities to the artist in so far as they tend to make some beliefs prevalent or stable.

An ideology is not a harmonious structure of beliefs or assumptions; some of its beliefs militate against others, and some of its standards militate against our nature. An ideology is an aggregate of beliefs sufficiently at odds with one another to justify opposite kinds of conduct. Thus, the artist's patterns of experience may be manifest in his particular stressing of the ideology. Accepting certain assumptions or beliefs as valid, he will exploit them to discredit other assumptions or beliefs which he considers invalid. He may, for instance, exploit assumptions of individual dignity to attack the assumptions that we must without protest obey the king. He may use the assumptions of natural beauty to rout the industrialist's assumptions of progress—or vice versa. It is by such aligning of assumptions that poetry contributes to the formation of attitudes, and thus to the determining of conduct.

26. *The Symbolically and formally "charged."* Intensity in art may be attributed sometimes to form, sometimes to the Symbol, sometimes to both. Symbolic intensity arises when the artist uses subject-matter "charged" by the reader's situation outside the work of art. Thus: the portrait of a spy in war times—the account of a seduction, in books for adolescents. (It is told that when Spain was lethargically enduring an unpopular dictatorship, and had suffered for several

years without rebellion, a vaudeville actor in a Madrid theatre opened his act by having the curtain rise on an empty
stage. The stage remained empty for some time, while the
audience grew more and more impatient. Finally, when they
were protesting furiously, the actor appeared. He held up his
hand for silence; the audience subsided; and he spoke rebuk-
ingly: "I don't see why you couldn't wait a few minutes. You
have been waiting now for seven years." This remark was
Symbolically "charged." Its ominous humor depended upon
a current political situation in Spain. Alter the situation of
the audience, and the witticism falls flat, becoming almost
meaningless.) Often, to "charge" his work Symbolically, a
writer strains to imagine some excessive horror, not because
he is especially addicted to such imaginings, but because the
prevalence of similar but less extreme Symbols has impaired
their effectiveness. He may plumb the depths of sadism or
incest when seeking no more than what an earlier writer
sought in the tale of a naïve courtship. If he would avoid the
procedure, he must Symbolize new patterns, or use new
modes of experience in the Symbolizing of old patterns, or
attempt to increase accuracy and range. To an extent, all
subject-matter is categorically "charged," in that each word
relies for its meaning upon a social context, and thus possesses values independently of the work in which it appears.
Symbolic charge, therefore, is but a matter of degree.

Formal charges may be attributed to arrangements within
the work itself. Though a writer were to feel dismal but
seldom, if he had stored the many aspects of his dismalness
and put them into a single work, such use of repetitive form
could give the impression of a world corroded by dismalness
from morning till night. Or if a writer so arranges his plot
that the words "I am here" have a pronounced bearing upon
the course of his story, the utterance of these simple words
may have a tremendous influence upon the audience. Con-

sider, in Racine's *Iphigénie,* the speech of Arcas, when he enters to announce that the time for Iphigenia's sacrifice is at hand. Up to this point, Iphigenia has been making arrangements for her marriage; she, her mother, her suitor, and her rival now learn for the first time that she is not to be married, but to be slain. The function of syllogistic progression in "charging" the words of Arcas is obvious.

As for the clear collaboration of both formal and Symbolic charge:

The description of a terrific storm is Symbolically charged. It relies for its effect upon our attitudes towards storms independently of the particular work in which this description appears. But, through the workings of qualitative progression, the description of a terrific storm may become more imposing if it follows, say, the account of a very effete scene in a salon. Or an image suggesting the vastness of a mountain may be reinforced by a peculiarity of rhythm, by a stressing of assonance, or by some saliency in the word-order. (The two kinds of charge, of course, are never wholly separable.)

27. *Eloquence.* Eloquence is a frequency of Symbolic and formal effects. One work is more eloquent than another if it contains Symbolic and formal charges in greater profusion. That work would be most eloquent in which each line had some image or statement relying strongly upon our experience outside the work of art, and in which each image or statement had a pronounced formal saliency.

We might contrast Stendhal and Shakespeare. The Symbol underlying *Le Rouge et le Noir* owes much of its effectiveness to its summarizing of certain volitionalist doctrines which were incipient in Stendhal's day but have since come to fruition. Also, the work in which this Symbol appears is marked by an exceptionally capable handling of repetitive form and syllogistic progression. The individual lines, how-

ever, are by definite program "non-eloquent." For their effect
they depend entirely upon their place in the whole. A conversation in Stendhal is not interesting as conversation; it is
interesting exactly as a conversation might be interesting in
real life: because of its bearing upon the future. It is interesting as an actual quarrel between two lovers might be
interesting to themselves—not because a single phrase of any
brilliance was spoken, but because each sentence was important to the lovers' relationship. Each sentence in Stendhal
deliberately eschews any saliency as a minor or incidental
form—it aims to be imperceptible—and if the reader forgets
that he is reading, he is reading as Stendhal would have him
read.

The "eloquent" principle, as exemplified by Shakespeare,
is a constant attempt to renew Symbolic and formal appeal
throughout the work. Each ramification of the Symbol must
depend for its effectiveness not merely upon its function as
a subdivision of the Symbol (repetitive form)—it must be
an image or statement containing Symbolic appeal in itself.
It must, that is, bring up some picture, or summarize some
situation, or in some other way recommend itself as an independent value. Or it must contain some oddity of sound or
rhythm which gives it an independent claim to our attention. Thus, by the principle of "eloquence," a conversation
would not merely reiterate the identity of the speakers and
contribute to the course of the plot—it would also be interesting as conversation.

28. *Manner and Style.* In so far as a work becomes eloquent, it manifests either manner or style. Here again the
distinction is quantitative, manner being a greater confinement of formal resources and Symbolic ramifications. Oscar
Wilde's *Salome* is an example of manner. (The ramifications
of the Symbol have a very limited range, bearing almost

wholly upon the stressing of decadent desire. Formally, the work is a constant repetition of the *non-sequitur*: the significance of the characters' statements is brought out formally by the perverse refusal of these characters to answer one another—they converse, but in monologue, and the most important questions are followed by an abrupt changing of the subject as the person replying pursues his own line of thought.) As an instance of style, we might consider the later prose of Shakespeare, with its range of imagery and formulation, and its abundance of diverse incidental forms. (This style approaches manner in so far as it overemphasizes metaphor.)

Manner obviously has the virtue of "power," with the danger of monotony (*Salome* may illustrate both). Style has the virtue of "complexity," with the danger of diffusion. (The later prose of James Joyce is a good instance of style impaired by diffusion.)

29. *The "categorical appeal" of literature.* Eloquence, by stressing the means of literature, requires an interest in the means as ends. Otherwise eloquence becomes an obstacle to enjoyment. Readers who seek in art a substitute for living will find the Stendhal procedure most acceptable; a novelist like the Hugo of *L'Homme Qui Rit* will annoy them with his bristling epigrammatic "unreality," a kind of saliency so thoroughly literary that, however strong the readers' impressions, they can never forget that the book is "written." Nor would Hugo want us to forget that his book was "written." The primary purpose of eloquence is not to enable us to live our lives on paper—it is to convert life into its most thorough verbal equivalent. The categorical appeal of literature resides in a liking for verbalization as such, just as the categorical appeal of music resides in a liking for musical sounds as such. The stressing of a medium requires a preference for

this medium—and thus in eloquence, which is the maximum stressing of the literary medium, we may find evidence of a "categorical appeal."

30. *"Æsthetic" truth.* The relation between "scientific" and "æsthetic" truth might be likened to the relation between revelation and ritual. Revelation is "scientific," whether its "truth" be founded upon magic, religion, or laboratory experiment. Revelation is "belief," or "fact." Art enters when this revelation is ritualized, when it is converted into a symbolic process. We treat with ceremony a fact considered of importance (if we consider a thing distinguished, we surround it with other things which we consider distinguished: we touch a "pure" object with "clean" hands). Art as eloquence, ceremony, ritual, is nothing other than this principle of consistency, of matching the important with the important. If the artist's "revelations" are of tremendous importance to him, he will necessarily seek to ritualize them, to find a correspondingly important setting for them.

But the ritualizing of a revelation does not merely produce revelation plus ritual. A kind of metaphorical truth enters. The artist, for instance, when he has converted his pattern of experience into a corresponding Symbol, finds himself with many problems which do not concern this pattern of experience at all. He will then treat this Symbol in ways which, from the standpoint of the underlying pattern, are "untrue." He may, for instance, though deeply opposed to religious dogma, write sympathetically of an imaginary religious service based wholly upon the most extreme kinds of dogma. Here truth is not "scientific," but "metaphorical." The "thoughts" of a writer are not the mere "revelation," not the statement of a fact—the "thoughts" are the framing of this revelation in ritual. Accordingly, our savants err who attempt to catalogue for us the "thoughts" of a stylist like Milton, by stating them simply as precepts divorced from their stylistic context. The "thoughts" of a writer are the non-paraphrasable aspects of his work, the revelation and the ritual in fusion. So greatly does the ritualistic element figure in the artist's mechanism, that he might rather ritualize a pattern of experience not wholly expressive of him than symbolize a pattern which he could not convert into ritual (as Mark Twain, who would preferably have been tragic, confined his formal writings to humor). It is this primary concern with "æsthetic" truth which has exposed the poet, even in his own eyes, to the charge of insincerity, and thus led him to attempt glorifying the charge. (The "insincerity" of putting one's children in an orphan asylum and writing a work on education—the "insincerity" of going to southern France and singing of Wisconsin—the "insincerity" of getting an effect by the use of an assumption which the artist himself often doubts.) A poet may base an effect upon a belief which he knows to be false, just as he may compose a poem on riding to the moon; in either case he writes "as if" the underlying fact were true.

Ritual, ceremony, eloquence, æsthetic truth, the non-paraphrasable, the metaphorical, the factually "insincere." (Ritual is to revelation as Lucretius is to Democritus. The "æsthetic truth" of Dr. Johnson's assertiveness becomes more apparent as the "scientific truth" of his assertions diminishes—Boswell's Johnson becomes a character out of Dickens.)

31. *Eloquence and the traditionally ceremonious.* The great danger in eloquence resides in the fact that it tends to become not a quantitative but a qualitative thing. The ritualizing of a revelation, that is, tends to confine itself to certain usages traditionally ceremonious. For if the artist would place his important revelation in an important setting, what more natural than that he should select for his setting such

ideas as are traditionally considered important? Eloquence thus comes to be allied with strict doctrines of inclusion and exclusion. It utilizes the traditionally dignified, overlooking the fact that any traditionally dignified word or image or "thought" is dignified not through an intrinsic quality but because earlier artists made it so. By laying emphasis upon the categorical appeal of art, eloquence threatens to make poetry "derivative," to make it develop out of itself rather than out of the situations of life. The poet thus derives his Symbolic charges from the Symbolic charges of his poetic forbears. In writing a "wouldst-thou" love poem today, the poet would be obtaining eloquence by the weakened method we have in mind, though the mistake is not always so obvious.

Eloquence, by our definition, would not be situated in such rigid distinctions between "good taste" and "bad taste." It would, rather, be a matter of profusion. The artist shows his respect for his subject, not by laying a wreath at its feet, but by the fulness of his preoccupation with it. The soundness of his concerns will be manifested either in exceptional variety or in exceptional accurateness. Now, if this profusion could be got from past literature alone, there could be no objection to so getting it. But it happens to require such intensity and spontaneity of purpose as can arise only out of situations in life itself. Thus, the artist whose eloquence is an eloquence of profusion, will base his inclusions and exclusions not on traditional definitions of the ceremonious, but upon those aspects of an ideology which can be associated with the ceremonious in his environment. His eloquence will be based upon the contemporaneously charged, rather than upon the traditionally charged. To an extent, of course, the contemporary charge will be a survival of the traditional—but there are new elements (in both ideology and "living") to which the traditional is not accurately adapted.

32. *Recurrent patterns of experience.* There are some stock patterns of experience which seem to arise out of any system of living. Thus: the dramatic irony of digging one's own grave (Bellerophontic letter); the return of youth (Faust legend, "the man who came back"); persecution at the hands of those whom one would benefit (Christ legend); slight cause leading to disproportionately grave effect ("The Piece of String"); Judas psychology (poignancy of harming a friend—Agamemnon sacrificing his daughter—Brutus conspiring against Cæsar for the good of the state); Utopia; *per aspera ad astra* (attainment after difficulty). One will find the Symbols for such patterns recurring throughout all literature. However, the Symbols, with their ramifications, vary greatly—and may not be effective though the underlying pattern applies strongly to the reader. Consider the many avid readers of the *per aspera ad astra* pattern as symbolized in our modern "success literature." Despite their eagerness, they would find little to entice them in this same pattern as symbolized by the *Quest of the Golden Fleece.* Pain at loss is universal—yet A will be greatly pained at the loss of something which B never had and never felt the need of having. Similarly, *Marius the Epicurean* and *The Doll's House* are concerned with fundamentally the same pattern—transition, the transvaluation of values. Ibsen symbolizes the pattern by modes of experience specifically applicable to the households of his audience. Pater symbolizes the pattern by modes of experience applicable to a post-Darwinian scholar of Græco-Roman classics. Though symbolizing a pattern of experience common to many, he symbolizes it by modes of experience exceptional to most. In both cases we have a pattern to which people in modern times are sensitive; yet the symbolizations of this pattern are so different that a certain kind of reader

could praise Ibsen for "dealing with life" and condemn Pater for "unreality." As the situation changes, the Pater Symbol may as likely as not be found the more apposite of the two, since it does not rely upon so specific a "charge" as the early feminist movement gave to Ibsen's Symbol.

Thus, though a pattern of experience could be proved universal (common to all men) or permanent (common to some men in every age), the work of art in which it is symbolized would not be thereby proved universal or permanent.

33. *Fluctuant factors affecting the Symbol.* The appeal of the Symbol may be impaired by the following factors:

Variations in ideology (an author, to make us admire a character, may endow the character with traits admirable by the author's code but not admirable by the reader's code. What Dickens considered the height of female virtue the reader may consider exceptional unimaginativeness. If picturing a sorry specimen of boyhood for Spartans, don't picture him as a thief.)

Remoteness of patterns (Baudelaire's preoccupations with purification through sin will have little to do with the preoccupations of a sales promoter at peace with his calling).

Divergence of modes (as illustrated by the Ibsen–Pater distinction, the different significance of snow to a Greenlander and snow to a Roman). Obviously, the line of demarcation between modes and patterns of experience is vague. A pattern is perhaps definable as a particular stressing of a mode. The details of life in the city would be *modes* of experience—a constant irritation at life in the city would be a *pattern* of experience. The modes would be the particular details with which this irritation was associated—as the irritation of a subway jam, of dodging automobiles, of early morning noises.

Degree of familiarity. (A Symbol may become ineffective,

not through any fundamental lack of appositeness, but simply because too many others have used the same Symbol. To sing hey-nonny-nonny effectively, one would now have to sing something else.) Also, the degree of familiarity with a pattern affects our judgment of the Symbol for this pattern. A person to whom the pattern is remote may need more obvious ramifications to be affected, whereas a person to whom the pattern is close might find many such obvious ramifications too blunt. (Contrast talk between two experts with talk between an expert and a layman. In talking with a layman, the expert will necessarily stress some of the very points which he would be most likely to omit in talking with another expert.)

34. *Formal obstacles.* We have previously indicated how progressive and repetitive form are affected by the casualties of subject-matter. Our analysis of eloquence (style and manner) now equips us to consider the possible alienation of readers through conventional form, or "categorical expectancy." Elizabethan audiences, through expecting the bluster of the proscenium speech, found it readily acceptable—but a modern audience not schooled in this expectation will object to it as "unreal." Yet this same audience will find nothing to resent in a kind of banter or smart repartee which is, so far as life itself is concerned, equally "unreal." The obstacle in conventional form arises from the fact that conventions militate against one another. The conventions of post-Ibsen drama, for instance, *do not merely omit* the Greek chorus; they *"demand" the omission* of the Greek chorus, one of the most effective mechanisms in the history of drama thereby being categorically eschewed.

The distinction between style and manner is also fluctuant, as a change in conventional form can make one aspect of a style very noticeable and thus give it the effect of manner. In the age of Pope, the metaphor of Shakespeare was disliked because of its conceptual weakness: in the interests of picturesqueness, it permitted itself to become intellectually inaccurate. The Imagists, on the other hand, disliked the Shakespearean metaphor because it was *too conceptual, too intellectual!* They preferred the suppression of the logical connectives which this metaphor always revealed. Thus to two other schools the Shakespearean metaphor, which was "natural" enough in its day, became an obstructive mannerism.

A maladjustment of conventional form can also arise from the pattern of experience. The reader who is, let us say, of a flighty, bustling nature, may require writing of the same sort. The diction "natural" to him will be composed of short, behavioristic sentences, with few modifiers. The leisurely, meditative manner of a Proust, or the complex solemnity of a De Quincey, will necessarily alienate him. He approaches art with a categorical demand for a specific kind of eloquence; which is to say, a pronounced pattern of experience will lead him to demand one specific manner of writing, and will by the same token make other manners or styles unsuitable to his enjoyment. Flaubert was pleased to think that he had accommodated his sentences to the human respiration, so that pauses fell at breathing spaces, though he did not specify whether he had in mind the short-breathed and apoplectic or the even respiratory performances of a trained singer. Most persons would be insensitive to any influence by such means, since they read with a minimum of auditory imaginings; but as for persons who may be sensitive to literary values of this kind, if Flaubert's respiratory pauses can give pleasure to a reader whose speed of breathing and reading corresponds with the speed to which the author's page is accommodated, for the same reason they might give displeasure to a reader in whom this correspondence was lacking.

35. *Compensatory gains*. A work, in ceasing to be apposite for the reasons previously described, need not thereby cease to appeal. There are extrinsic aspects of appeal. Thus, through the passing of Latin, Virgil takes on a sepulchral dignity not there for his contemporaries. Among such compensatory gains are: antiquity (the appeal of a work removed in time); quaintness (the appeal of a work removed in custom, or ideology); absurdity (the appeal of a work through its sheer error, the work being "efficient enough in its badness" to make a virtue of its defects); typicality (the appeal of a work because it is representative, or symptomatic, of certain critical theories, as the appeal of a work "because it is representative of nineteenth-century England"); rarity (the appeal of a work because there are few works of its kind); picturesqueness (appeal of an attitude which, being alien to the reader, furnishes him with a "fresh" way of seeing things. Thus, though the author be very guileless, if he happens to write out of a social or emotional situation greatly different from the reader's, his work may become the equivalent of great inventiveness or ingenuity. It is in this way that primitive works often appeal to us, delighting us as a vehicle for "artistic" effects, giving us the sense of the dextrous that we get in the depiction of Falstaff). In general, the work possesses extrinsic appeal when its appeal resides in the reader's failure to duplicate the experience intended by the author. (A "realistic" account of life in Tibet will appeal as a "romantic" book to Occidentals; what one man loves as doxology another may admire for its uniqueness.)

Again, works invalidated as "scientific" truth may take on appeal as "æsthetic" truth. The disproving of Democritus does not invalidate the doctrines of Democritus as "poetized" in Lucretius' *De Rerum Natura*. Plato and Spinoza, whose doctrines, in their literal meaning, are endangered, survive as "artists," their questioned "scientific" truth being em-

balmed as "æsthetic" truth. The blunt certainties of a Dr.
Johnson gain as "æsthetic" truth, the more thoroughly they
are undermined as "scientific" truth. One may enjoy these
certainties as a "tonic" for his many modern doubts. Thus,
though Johnson, as the Symbol of Boswell's *Life*, ceases to
appeal as the summarizing of a situation, he appeals as the
adjustment to a situation.

Similarly, conventional form can appeal through its sheer
divorce from contemporary expectations. The very reader
who would object if someone wrote today in the eighteenth-
century manner may find this manner of great appeal in an
eighteenth-century writer.

36. *Margin of persuasion.* "Compensatory gains" occur
when the Symbol appeals for reasons extrinsic to the author's
intentions. By the "margin of persuasion" we refer to the
means whereby the author can reduce the recalcitrant reader
to acquiescence, the means whereby the Symbol, though
remote from the reader, can be made to appeal for reasons
intrinsic to the author's intention.

First, there is the authority of the expert. The artist possessed by a certain pattern of experience is an "expert" in
this pattern. He should thus be equipped to make it convincing, for the duration of the fiction at least. By thoroughness he should be able to overwhelm his reader and thus
compel the reader to accept his interpretations. For a pattern
of experience is an interpretation of life. Life being open to
many interpretations, the reader is open to many interpretations. Only the madman or the genius or the temporarily
exalted (as the lover, the terrified, or the sick) will have a
pattern of experience so pronounced as to close him to the
authority of other patterns of experience. The thoroughness
of the artist's attack can "wear down" the reader until he
accepts the artist's interpretation, the pattern of experience

underlying the Symbol. He may, when the book is finished, return to his own contrary patterns of experience forthwith (but during the reading the evidence has been rigorously selected, it "points" as steadily in one direction as the contentions of a debater).

This "margin of persuasion" is further made possible by the fact that our modes of experience are ambiguous or fluctuant. That is, the normal person has a variety of feelings attached to the same object. A thunder-shower can cause terror if one is caught far from shore in a rowboat, or relief if it tempers the heat. A locomotive can cause terror if onrushing, or relief if it takes us away from an unsatisfactory environment. Thus the artist, who attempts to convey emotions by drawing upon the modes of experience connected with such emotions, could use locomotives and storms to convey emotions as unlike as terror and relief. Have the train onrushing, with a car stalled on the tracks in a violent downpour, and "storm-locomotive" conveys terror; have the hero break clear of his troubles by flight, have him settle back comfortably in a Pullman chair as the train moves quietly out of the station, with the storm, after the oppressive sultriness of the day, causing a cool wind to blow down the aisle, and "storm-locomotive" conveys relief. Thus, the fluctuant quality in our modes of experience provides a neutral or ambiguous territory which the artist can "weight," which he can by his selective methods endow with a pattern.

This neutral or ambiguous territory serves the artist in another way. Many of his sharpest perceptions, his most convincing images, or the most skilful trends in the treatment of his plots, are not exclusively allied with his particular pattern of experience. The same inventions could have arisen out of some other pattern of experience. Thus, the author can inveigle his reader by the rich use of this "neutral" territory. Byron may appeal to the Byronic by his Byronism—

but to a certain non-Byronic reader he may have to appeal, say, by such qualities of natural observation as ally him with Shelley.

We must also consider the value of formal appeal in inducing acquiescence. For to guide the reader's expectations is already to have some conquest over him. Thus even a rhythm not categorically adapted to the reader (he may prefer swifter ones or slower ones or more voluminous ones, etc.) can increase its adaptability through the patient pervasiveness of repetitive form.

The "margin of persuasion" is the region of corrosion, corrosion obtained by thoroughness, thoroughness manifest either as accuracy, or as profusion, or as both.

37. *Perfection.* Enough has been said to demonstrate that "perfection" as applied to literature is a meaningless term. The naturalness of progressive and repetitive form is impaired by divergence in the ideologies of writer and reader (the writer cannot arouse us to vindictiveness by an act which, though he considers it despicable, we happen to consider pitiable, as certain kinds of "wickedness" are now condoned as "insanity"). The work can very easily be maladjusted from the standpoint of conventional form, if it fails to coincide with our expectations (a work may have much stylistic vigor, but the very eloquence of the diction will militate against it if the reader "categorically" requires simple narrative statement). The hypertrophy or atrophy of any principle can be effective or obstructive, depending upon the bias of the reader. The same Symbol appeals to different readers for different reasons: (1) because there is a similarity of writer's and reader's pattern (a Byronic Symbol appealing to a "mute Byron"); or (2) because the writer by his thoroughness compels the reader to accept his interpretation (a Poe horror story making a joyous man feel uneasy); or (3)

by "compensatory gains" (as the free thinker De Gourmont delighted in the early poetry of the Church). Again, the pattern underlying the Symbol can be obscured by the modes of experience employed in the ramifying of the Symbol (songs about the merry month of May would hardly fit as a greeting to spring in Tierra del Fuego; one cannot awaken a sense of strangeness in the reader by talking of Xanadu, if the reader happens to be Kubla Khan).

Perfection could exist only if the entire range of the reader's and the writer's experience were identical down to the last detail. Universal and permanent perfection could exist only if this entire range of experiences were identical for all men forever.

To have "perfection," we should need a "perfect reader" to whom such perfection could be referred. That is, we should have to specify some definite pattern of experience as the "ideal" pattern of experience. Should a warlike work of art, for instance, be so written as to stir the patriotic, or so written as to stir the anti-patriotic (in the first case we might arouse the audience by depicting the brutalities of the national enemy, in the second we might arouse the audience by depicting the machinations of our own munitions makers). Should the work of art appeal to the humiliated, the indignant, the suffering—or should it appeal to those who, either by good fortune or by some deep "philosophy," have acquired repose? Obviously, the work of art can appeal to either—and in appealing most fully to one, it prejudices its appeal to the other. Reducing the problem to its simplest terms, Aristotle points out in his *Rhetoric* that there are friendly audiences, hostile audiences, and simply curious audiences, the orator's problems differing in accordance with the type of audience he is addressing. Such divisions apply as rigorously to the Symbols of poetry and fiction as to any subjects of abstract debate. To speak of a work as "perfect," we should have to establish one of these audiences as the point of reference.

As a kind of hypothetical norm, we might divide our readers into the "hysteric" and the "connoisseur." The hysteric will demand in art a Symbol which is "medicinal" to his situation. He will require one very specific kind of art. In so far as the reader approaches the hypothetical state of the connoisseur, he is open to the appeal of all Symbols, but is overwhelmed by none. He will approach art *as art*, thus requiring the maximum of ritualization, verbalization. He will be "will-less," "hunger-less," going to art for nothing but art itself. He will require not one specific kind of art (as the hysteric, who must have only detective stories, or murder stories, or success fiction) but any art profuse in technical happenings. The actual reader is obviously an indeterminate and fluctuant mixture of these two extremes. An art might be said to approach "perfection" in proportion as its appeal is made to the second kind of reader—but in all purity he could not possibly exist. Every word a writer uses depends for its very "meaning" upon the reader's previous experience with the object or situation which this word suggests. That is to say, the word is "charged" by the reader's own experiences, and to this extent the reader is "hysteric." "Madness" is but meaning carried to the extreme.

Or we might limit the matter, calling a work perfect if it attains its ends—a patriotic work being in a broad sense perfect if it is written for patriots and moves patriots, and an anti-patriotic play being perfect if it is written for anti-patriots and moves anti-patriots. (For those who would say that the anti-patriotic play can also move patriots, I should but ask them to consider producing such a play in war times. It can move patriots in times of peace, *when their patriotism has weakened*: in other words, it can move them in so far as they are *not* patriots.) Thus, we can only preserve "perfection" in this sense: "a perfect work for girls of seventeen who are living in small provincial towns in 1931 are not very well educated, are dissatisfied with their surroundings, and dream of a career in Hollywood," or "a perfect work for people with six toes, this spring." We can save the concept of perfection only by making it of no critical value. If a work of art were perfectly adapted to one situation, by this very fact its chances of subsequent perfection would be eliminated, as the identical situation will not recur.

38. *"Literary virtues."* (Recapitulation.) The virtues of the poet may be discussed as

Eloquence: Vigor of Symbolic and formal "charging." Thoroughness (as exemplified intensively in accuracy and extensively in profusion).

Power and complexity (of the Symbol, of the pattern underlying the Symbol): Powerful Symbol for a powerful pattern (*Othello*); complex Symbol for a complex pattern (*Hamlet*); complex Symbol for a powerful pattern (Proust?); powerful Symbol for a complex pattern (Aschenbach of Mann's *Death in Venice*). The last type frequently characterizes the great "simple" lyric, which suggests in a few lines a complex situation capable of exhaustive novelistic analysis.

Manner: Power without monotony. Restriction of the means by which formal and Symbolic saliency is obtained. (A mannerism is a particular means of acquiring saliency which happens to strike the reader as protrusive.)

Style: Complexity without diffusion. Diffusion may be decorative (excess variety). Diffusion may also be simply the lack of pronounced identity (as in the prose of mere statement, or information-giving board reports, news items, grocery orders).

"Specific needs" versus "categorical needs" of art: Shakespeare meets the "needs" of people who want poetic drama (categorical needs). Many a contemporary novel meets the

"needs," say, of people who want to see life in Paris cafés (specific needs).

39. *Uplift. How eloquence leads to uplift:* The profuse embodiment of eloquence cannot be accomplished without coexisting discipline (resistance) and exposure (non-resistance). The poet must manage exposure without collapse, discipline without exclusion. The artist does, of course, tend to develop a "protective" attitude, and he may be content to symbolize it. But in attempting to increase the range of his arguments (the thoroughness of his ramifications), he is pledged to the deepening and widening of his patterns and to the strengthening of his formal contrivances. The expansion of the Symbol, since it is done for the purpose of appeal, involves processes of intellection, or logic (hence the difference between the *passivity* of a dream and the *enterprise* of art).

Value of the aggregate: The great mass of art can produce an effect beyond the range of the individual artists. Were each artist to give us but a restricted pattern, we could get something beyond these experiences out of their assemblage, owing to the conflicts and mutual exclusions. For the sincere artist, the pattern is, within the terms of the fiction at least, as he writes it. For the reader the artist's world may become, at the termination of the fiction, a mere addition to his working hypotheses. The "sum total of art" relieves the artist of the need of seeing life steadily and seeing it whole. He will presumably desire to be as comprehensive as he can, but what he lacks in adjustability can be supplied by another artist affirming some other pattern with equal conviction.

Technical: The exercise of human subtleties and potentialities in a sphere which can be largely non-competitive. Increase of perception and sensitivity through increase of terminology (a character or a situation in fiction is as much a term as any definition in a scientific nomenclature). An equipment, like any vocabulary, for handling the complexities of living.

Holier than thou: The artist, as artist, will be more concerned with moral imaginings than with moral stability. He must, of course, be able to perceive his refinements for the duration of the saying—but character, in the social sense, is based upon an integrity, or constancy, which an artist—as artist—need not have. If art were a matter of character, rather than of artistic aptitude, it follows that a great painter would also be a great musician, a great novelist, a great architect, etc. Perhaps no man can, by taking thought, add a cubit to his stature; but he clearly can, by revision, remove much that lowers his general average. So we may consider art as bigger than the artist, who can accordingly apply himself to his trade in its noblest aspects with such modesty as befits any standard of human decency. For if the calling is greater than the man, he need not, in the selection of so high a calling, feel himself in the coxcomb's position of standing forth as a moral muster for all mankind.

APPLICATIONS OF THE
TERMINOLOGY

Hierarchy. Many aspects of a writer's merit, being wholly outside him, change independently of him (as is particularly the case with the changes in ideology and in the predominant aspects of a social situation). Every poem is, in a sense, an "occasional" poem — and it is somewhat a matter of accident whether the occasion for which the poem was written continues frequently to recur. (Or, for that matter, the situation for which a work is written may become more widespread at a later date than at the time of its production, in which case the work may seem to a later age more apropos than it did to its own. This eventuality likewise may be more to a writer's good fortune than to his credit.) In asking that literature produce one sort of effect rather than another, we should be asking that literature fit one sort of situation rather than another.[1]

There are two general bases of critical exhortation. (1) We may have a concept of an ideal situation, and insist that literature be written in accordance with this ideal situation; or (2) we may have a concept of a contemporary situation, and insist that literature be written in accordance with this contemporary situation. The first method is absolutist: it seeks to determine once and for all what kind of literature is categorically superior to what other kinds of literature. The second method is relativistic, or historical: it holds that

---

[1] A work may be said to "fit" a situation in two ways. It may fit as a corrective to the situation—or it may be said to "fit" simply because the situation enables it to be well received. The two ways are not necessarily opposed, but are often opposed.

if literature is to be written for an ideal situation at a time when the actual situation is far from ideal, writers must sacrifice the appositeness of art in the interests of a purely academic concept of "perfection." The first method would decide *in absoluto* whether literature should provide bread or cake; the second method would have to say "sometimes bread—sometimes cake, according to the 'needs' at the particular moment." The second method may seem, on the face of it, more readily defensible—but it has difficulties of its own, and though all the absolutists were silenced, there would still be endless bickerings among the relativists, since a given situation can be interpreted in many ways, and thus may be shown to have diametrically opposite "needs." In one respect, however, the advocates of the second method now have the advantage: the advocates of the first method, while holding to the categorical superiority of some literature (as the Neo-Humanists), have yielded much to the ways of historical or relativistic thinking, and have sought to defend their brands of art, not solely in accordance with a concept of perfection, but also as being apposite to the contemporary scene. Yet a particular brand of art cannot be at once categorically superior and best fitted for all situations in history, since the situations in history change so greatly that, by being better fitted to deal with one, a brand of art would necessarily be worse fitted for dealing with others.

Thus, some absolutist critics, having hit upon a distinction between "yea-saying" and "nay-saying," ask that literature be not a protest, but an affirmation. But who says "yea" badly has nay-said—and one is almost certain to say "yea" badly if he and his contemporaries are living in a pig-sty. In so far as we may look upon literature as an incipient form of action (in the pitting of some assumptions against others, the poet leaves us with an implied code of conduct), we might reasonably expect literature to say "yea" or "nay" purely in accordance with the kind of action demanded by the times. We do not categorically praise one remedy above another unless both are intended to cure the same illness in the same type of patient. And in so far as life is a solving of problems, to praise categorically a certain kind of solution (a certain brand of art) is to praise a method regardless of the problem (which would be like advocating the use of nothing but quadratic equations, though the problem to be solved had no concern with quadratic equations—nor is the analogy so far-fetched, as there are certain kinds of honest outcry to which the tests of "affirmation" are totally irrelevant).

The last decade has counted many attacks upon Rousseau. Rousseau's principles, according to his modern opponents, have led to vast absurdities. Let us, to simplify the issue, grant their contentions, though there are many who would attribute our difficulties to too little Rousseau rather than to too much. But even if we granted the contentions of his opponents, we should not overlook the fact that any principles can lead to vast absurdities, if only because principles persist and grow in popularity long after they have gained the end for which they were formulated. And in outlasting their original beneficent function, they take on a maleficent function, for instead of running counter to the situation which they were designed to correct, they may now be carrying to excess the situation which they served to bring about. Indeed, we might almost say that the predominance of a principle is *per se* evidence that this principle has outlived its usefulness; for by the time it has penetrated from the busy centers of thought to the sluggish periphery of mankind, the situation for which it was designed has certainly altered.

As for the "classic-romantic" dichotomy, and the many feuds arising from the attempt first to make such distinctions and then to plead for one school at the expense of the other, we might attempt a distinction of our own, based upon a slightly different definition of dualistic and monistic thinking. The classicists have, in general, praised dualistic thought, conceiving of the individual as the balancing of opposite principles, and they have accused the romantic of being monistic, or one-sided. They have pointed out that a monistic principle contains no basis of correction—that its "logical conclusion" is not distinguishable from its "reduction to absurdity." The romantic, however, can likewise lay claim to a dualistic system, having for opposites the principle which he stands for and the principle represented by the society against which he revolts. His "individualism" never for a moment permits him to forget the "enemy"—and indeed, to be effective, he must have a great understanding of the "enemy," must to an extent encompass the "enemy."

It seems that, at a time when many people are living dissatisfactorily, the romantic dualism (of "oneself against society") will be the more useful mode of correction (as one "establishes his equilibrium by leaning"). Classicism, however, would seem particularly useful at precisely that time when a monistic principle has come to have considerable weight against the "opposition" and is threatening to become the predominant influence in turn. At this point classicism might serve to hold the two principles in fusion, to prevent as long as possible either from gaining upon the other. Classicism might thus be called the flowering of a romantic excess. The nature of its insight is determined by the romantic emphases out of which it arises. When the battle has been fought, it can attempt to prolong the amenities of peace.

So much for the two under ideal conditions. Each can be misused. We can have classicists, extolling affirmation and poise, when a small class happens to be enjoying a privileged way of life out of which much order and charm can be extracted by the fortunate. We can have romantics, calling for rebellion, simply because their morbid vanity has been injured. The weaknesses of each position have been soundly attacked by the members of the other camp. But as for the entire picture of the two types (classic "repose" and romantic "disturbance") we must realize that either represents a selection from the normal experiences of a day, which have both their classic and romantic aspects. "Poise" and "decorum" are as much an arbitrary simplification as "rebellion," and it is only by denying some aspects of our day that we could categorically rule out one type in favor of the other.

Art and "Life." The exhortation that the artist "deal with life" is confusing, particularly as it is hard to understand how he could deal with anything else. When applied to novels, the slogan seems to mean that the artist should give us characters which seem "life-like," should show them doing things which seem "natural," and should tell his tale in a simple, running style which is unobtrusive and permits the reader to follow it unawares. Yet, however strongly critics insist that these be the traits of the novel, they are not the traits of lyric poetry, and thus are not always essential to the process of "dealing with life." The fact is that much of the world's greatest literature lacks the "life-like" characters and the "natural" actions and the "conversational" manner which one can find, or thinks he can find, in even inferior fictions of the nineteenth century. To this extent, therefore, we may seem justified in interpreting the exhortation to "deal with life" as an exhortation to preserve certain conventions of nineteenth-century prose fiction.

Other critics mean by the phrase "deal with life" that the artist should deal with specific "problems" of the day. Thus, we have the proletarian critic, who asks that the writer never close his eyes to labor disputes, slum conditions, political outrages, etc. "Dealing with life," by this system, usually contains all the requirements listed above, plus an attack upon the "evasiveness" of a writer who devotes himself, say, to historical idylls depicting the life of the cultured rich on Greek islands of antiquity. The proletarian critic will call such an idyll bourgeois literature of "escape." He will say that it is welcomed by bourgeois readers because its phantasy enables them to forget the harsh realities underlying their prosperity. Incidentally, in pursuing such a line of attack he overlooks entirely the effect which a "Utopian" literature may have in sharpening a reader's dissatisfaction with the contemporary scene. For the very book that may serve a reader as an "evasion" while he is reading it, may make reality seem all the more unappealing when he is not reading (psychoanalysis having led us to forget how, but a few years ago, the "escape" literature of love romances was condemned by educators, not because it enabled the readers to "accept" the world as it was, but because by contrast it made the facts of everyday life very unacceptable).

Underlying the proletarian attitude is the assumption that literature must be "useful," that it must serve to eradicate certain forms of social injustice, and that it can eradicate these forms of injustice only by dealing with them specifically. It overlooks entirely the fact that there is the pamphlet, the political tract, the soap-box oration, to deal with the specific issues of the day, whereas the literature of the imagination may prepare the mind in a more general fashion. That is, a great work, dealing with some hypothetical event remote in history and "immediacy," may leave us with a desire for justice—and the political speaker may profit by this equipment when he shows his hearers that some particular situation in his particular precinct is unjust. There must be a literature which upholds such an equipment in the abstract, if the social reformer is to find something in us to which he can appeal when advocating reforms in the particular. It is fortunate for the proletarian reformer that so much of art is written in defiance of his injunctions.[2]

Again, by the exhortation that literature "deal with life," we often mean that literature should be popular. For it is obvious that if a book engrosses one reader, it has "dealt with life" so far as he is concerned, though all the rest of mankind find it trivial and unconvincing. Accordingly if, knowing that a book has in the present or past engrossed a few readers, we insist that it does not deal with life, we must mean that it should engross more readers.

To consider the entire issue from the standpoint of the "Lexicon":

A writer is engaged in the producing of effects upon his readers. He may seek to produce such effects as appeal to a large audience, or to a small audience, or to a particular kind of audience (as an audience of workingmen, or an audience of scholars). Thus he will aim to produce the sort of effects which certain people (presumably more or less like himself) will find appealing. He will manipulate their ideology, he will exploit his and their own patterns of experience, he will symbolize by one set of modes or another (he may prey upon their sense of injustice, for instance, by depicting the maltreatment of a slave on a Greek island of antiquity, or by an account of child labor conditions in the cotton mills—and whether he use the "antique" modes or the "modern," he is

---

[2] In one respect, however, art may serve his purposes very well. If a political doctrine which he advocates is repugnant to most people, the artist may "naturalize" it by depicting very humane types of people who hold to this doctrine (thus pitting the reader's assumptions as to "likable people" against his assumptions as to the degradation of the doctrine). Such a procedure militates against a naïve but basic tendency on the part of mankind to associate an abhorrent doctrine with one specific kind of abhorrent person (an association which probably explains why nearly every heretic sect was generously credited with "unnatural practices," as are the victims of morphine today).

dealing with life if he awakens in his readers such rage against injustice as he intended to awaken).

A work deals with life for a great many people when it symbolizes such patterns of experience as characterize a great many people and ramifies the Symbol by such modes of experience as appeal to a great many people. It may, in so doing, prove its unfitness to deal with life for others, who require other kinds of Symbolization and who happen— whether through their way of living or through the conventions of their art—to demand that the Symbols be ramified in other modes of experience. A fiction designed for an audience of workingmen, for instance, may give such pictures of life among the wealthy as could never be said by the wealthy to deal with life. But these pictures, however inaccurate, "deal with life" so long as they serve as Symbols for arousing in the workingmen such emotions as the artist wished to arouse. One must realize that many works of the past which now seem "hollow" are hollow because they were so well adapted to "dealing with life" under their particular set of conditions (they were "occasional poems" for occasions so specific that the occasions are not likely to recur). We may further recall our account of the vaudeville actor's witticism in Spain ("Lexicon": Topic 26, "The Symbolically and formally 'charged'"). Transferred to America at present, the witticism would be completely "hollow." But the day may come when we too have been "waiting for seven years." The witticism will then "deal with life." We must realize, on this point, that when to "deal with life" means to exploit "burning issues" (as the popular magazines often attempt to do) the author is choosing the readiest means of producing his effects, the means which happen to be most effective at the moment (as would a playwright "exposing" vice conditions at a time when the public was much exercised over a crusade against vice rings).

COUNTER-STATEMENT

In conclusion: The most "unreal" book in the world can properly be said to "deal with life" if it can engross a reader (that is, if it is an "occasional poem" written for the particular sort of occasion which happens to characterize the reader's own life or stage of life). Some ages will prefer (as in the time of Lyly) such persiflage and gallantry as never was. But we must not overlook the fact that, however "artificial" such a style may be, the feeling behind it, the love of ceremony which it symbolizes, is as "natural" and "spontaneous" as any other emotion. For many people the emphases of today may be such that this love of ceremony seems trifling and malapropos; for them, not only the exaggerated *désinvolture* of a Lyly, but even the fluent badinage of Restoration Comedy, will seem not to "deal with life." And the author who would get general credit for "dealing with life" must give more attention to other emphases, other forms of the conventional and unreal which happen at the moment to be deemed more "natural."

Objective-subjective. In the "great ages," when drama flourishes, art is "objective." That is, the artist gets his effects primarily by the exploitation of the current ideology. In the society of the times there are many implicit judgments, a general agreement as to what is heroic, what cowardly, what irreligious, what boorish, what clever, etc.—the playwright thus being able to affect his audience by endowing his characters with these various traits. The advantages of such a method are obvious. The artist may easily obtain the maximum of "impersonality." If he is at peace with the world, he may manipulate those aspects of the current ideology which make for comedy; if he is gloomy, he may exploit the implicit judgments of the day to produce tragedy; but, beyond this, his personal bias need not intrude at all.

Racine's prefaces to his plays illustrate to perfection the

"objective" method of composition. They disclose how, using the contemporary ideology of vice and virtue, of nobility and disgrace, he would put a character together almost like mixing the ingredients in a cooking recipe, balancing vices and virtues, sympathetic and antipathetic traits, purely from the standpoint of the attitude which he intended to arouse in his audience. Thus: "In Euripides and Seneca, Hippolyte is accused of actually violating his mother-in-law: *vim corpus tulit*. But here he is accused of only having entertained the thought. I wanted to spare Thésée a confusion which would have made him less appealing to the audience." Or again: "As for the character of Hippolyte, I noticed that ancient writers blamed Euripides for having depicted him as a philosopher so free of all imperfections that the death of this young prince aroused much more indignation than pity. I thought that I should give him some weakness which would make him somewhat guilty towards his father, though without taking from him any of that magnanimity with which he protects the honor of Phèdre and accepts suffering rather than accuse her. I consider as weakness the passion which he felt in spite of himself for Aricie, who is the daughter and the sister of his father's mortal enemies." Or of Phèdre: "I am not surprised that this character had so happy a success in the days of Euripides, and that it has still succeeded so well in our era, since it has all the qualities which Aristotle requires of the tragic hero, and which are adapted to the arousing of pity and terror." And of the play *Iphigénie*: "Thus the outcome of the play is drawn from its very foundations; and one has but to see it acted to realize what pleasure I have provided for the audience, both by saving at the end a virtuous princess in whom the audience has come to take such an interest during the course of the tragedy, and in saving her by some other means than by a miracle [i.e., the *deus ex machina*] which the audience could not have accepted because they could not have believed in it." [3]

This dramatic or objective method (of composing one's symbols from the standpoint of the effect desired) is weakened in proportion as the ideology which the dramatist relies upon is weakened. And in time an ideology must weaken, either through processes of exhaustion, or through the encroachment of new material which the ideology cannot encompass. As this weakening progresses, the artist will necessarily become less "objective." On finding the ideology impaired, he will look for some other kind of certainty to take the place of it. He will, in art, search for something which is equivalent to Descartes' *"cogito, ergo sum"* in metaphysics; he will, that is, tend to found his art upon an irreducible minimum of belief. This irreducible minimum is, obviously, his personal range of experiences, his own exaltations and depressions, his specific kinds of triumph and difficulty. Wherefore, he will tend to symbolize his particular "pattern of experience"—his art will become "subjective." Some critics will decry this development as a kind of self-indulgence on the part of the artist: but they might with equal justice salute the accuracy of the artist in making the change. In any event, the most vigorous and enterprising artists will be found to be the ones who have manifested this "subjective" tendency most thoroughly, while the hackmen, the Broadway playwrights and the writers of purely commercial fiction, will be found to rely greatly upon the remaining vestiges of the ideology (often they use aspects of the ideology which, though brought into confusion by new matter, still flourish in "backwoods of the mind" not yet affected by the force of the new matter; and just as often they exploit certainties of

[3] Perhaps we should mention, as a particular instance of Racine's manipulation of the ideology current in his times, his great reliance upon the concepts of honor which distinguished the "æsthetic" of the court.

the moment, as a financial panic, or a wave of patriotism in war times—among this group being also those objective writers who have, in recent years, been working the vein of "youthful sophistication").

In summary: the objective writer attempts to make effective Symbols; the subjective writer attempts to make Symbols effective (that is, constructs a Symbol as the replica of his own pattern of experience, and having constructed it, schemes to find ways of making it effective).

The distinction might throw some light upon the "enigma of *Hamlet*." Shakespeare, as dramatist at a time when an ideology was flourishing (consider, for instance, what advantages the author of *Othello* had over a modern playwright who, under the disturbances of recent psychological tenets, would attempt a tragedy of jealousy built upon a concept of chastity), was adept at the composition of effective Symbols. His plays were constructed from the standpoint of the effect to be produced; and with the exception of *Hamlet,* when a character in Shakespeare becomes "enigmatic," or unusually complex, we can account for the phenomenon by discovering that Shakespeare has stretched the mold of the character slightly in order to gain some momentary theatrical effect. That is, he seems to feel that the theatrical effect will be startling enough and engrossing enough in itself to make the audience overlook the fact that the consistency of the character is somewhat violated (a trick which would probably have remained undisclosed had not so many patient scholars taken to studying the characters as characters, and gone to painful lengths in trying to explain away inconsistencies which can readily be explained from the standpoint of dramatic expediency). In the case of Hamlet, however, the matter is different. There are diffuse and confusing aspects of Hamlet which cannot be explained from the standpoint of a desired effect, for the effect itself is muddled. Was

Hamlet constructed in the "subjective," "non-dramatic" manner? Does he symbolize a specific pattern of experience? Did Shakespeare, for one reason or another, renounce the dramatist's method? Mr. Eliot has noted the similarity between this play and the sonnets. Could we not carry the similarity to the point of noting the non-dramatic element in both, the predominant characteristic shared by both as Symbols of a pattern—with the one notable difference that *Hamlet* is a product of the author's maturity? If the Symbol of Hamlet was developed, not from the standpoint of effectiveness, but as the reduplication of a pattern, we should have some explanation for the hypertrophied "character-depiction" of, let us say, Act II, Scene 2, with its obvious complaining and settling of "personal scores" outside the limits of the fiction.

It is, of course, no new thing to "explain" Hamlet as Shakespeare. Our distinction might simply make more precise the nature of Hamlet's "failure." Some private difficulties, we may suppose, became so intense that, despite the flourishing of the ideology, Shakespeare for once could not content himself with merely arousing tragic feelings—he had to symbolize the pattern of his own particular tragedy. Mr. Eliot has suggested that Shakespeare may, at this time, have read Montaigne—a very acute suggestion, since it may be true in essence whether or not it is true in actuality. For in this play Shakespeare shows a tendency towards the least dramatic of all ways of thinking, the "essayistic." The essayist, in contrast with the dramatist, can dispense with a maximum of certainty in ideology. If a code is crumbling he can, with all the convenience in the world, say so. Whereas the dramatist exploits beliefs, the essayist can devote himself precisely to the questioning of beliefs. And it is at least an interesting accident that in this play, where the playwright displays something very close to bafflement, his protagonist states with resignation: "Why, then, 'tis none to you; for there is nothing either good or bad, but thinking makes it so," a thought which undermines the very foundations of a dramatist, since it suggests that he is getting his effects out of an almost gratuitous or arbitrary ideology, and that subsequent impairments of the ideology—which are totally beyond his management—may imperil the vigor of his results.

There is evidence that in this, the most "subjective" of Shakespeare's plays, the playwright's confusions were both practical and æsthetic, that the bleakness of his outlook arose from a concomitant questioning of both his life and his artistic methods. Such a double difficulty would be sufficient to overwhelm any man, and force him into "personal complaint," the symbolizing of his experiential pattern.

At a later date, however, when the ideology of our culture was threatening to disintegrate under the effect of many new influences brought to bear upon it, a writer would not require such great personal stress to embrace the literature of "confession," the subjective. We may suppose that a skilled dramatist, writing at a time when an ideology was intact, could be induced only under pressure of great anguish to symbolize a specific pattern of experience—whereas this readjustment could be accepted by artists of a later age with almost no discomfiture whatever, since they had never found the ideology powerful enough for them to build a method upon its full utilization.[4]

[4] This is not offered as an alternative explanation to Mr. Eliot's. As a matter of fact, I believe that it is little more than Mr. Eliot's explanation rephrased. As stated in *The Sacred Wood* the argument runs: "The only way of expressing emotion in the form of art is by finding an 'objective correlative'; in other words, a set of objects, a situation, a chain of events which shall be the formula of that *particular* emotion; such that when the external facts, which must terminate in sensory experience, are given, the emotion is immediately evoked. If you examine any of Shakespeare's more successful trag-

COUNTER-STATEMENT

Poetry and Illusion. Since certain things were believed, and poets used these beliefs to produce poetic effects, the beliefs became "poetic." But in the course of time contrary things came to be believed, with the consequence that the earlier beliefs were now called "illusions." And noting that so much of the world's poetry had been built upon what were now called illusions, the critics argued in a circle: The illusions, they said, were poetic, and in the loss of the illusions

edies, you will find this exact equivalence; you will find that the state of mind of Lady Macbeth walking in her sleep has been communicated to you by a skilful accumulation of imagined sensory impressions; the words of Macbeth on hearing of his wife's death strike us as if, given the sequence of events, these words were automatically released by the last event in the series. The artistic 'inevitability' lies in this complete adequacy of the external to the emotion; and this is precisely what is deficient in *Hamlet*. Hamlet (the man) is dominated by an emotion which is inexpressible, because it is in *excess* of the facts as they appear. And the supposed identity of Hamlet with his author is genuine to this point: that Hamlet's bafflement at the absence of objective equivalent to his feelings is a prolongation of the bafflement of his creator in the face of his artistic problem. Hamlet is up against the difficulty that his disgust is occasioned by his mother, but that his mother is not an adequate equivalent for it; his disgust envelops and exceeds her. It is thus a feeling which he cannot understand; he cannot objectify it, and it therefore remains to poison life and obstruct action. . . . To have heightened the criminality of Gertruda would have been to provide the formula for a totally different emotion in Hamlet; it is just *because* her character is so negative and insignificant that she arouses in Hamlet the feeling which she is incapable of representing." Thus, Mr. Eliot concludes: "We must simply admit that here Shakespeare tackled a problem which proved too much for him. Why he attempted it at all is an insoluble puzzle; under compulsion of what experience he attempted to express the inexpressibly horrible, we cannot ever know. . . ." Agreed, that we probably "cannot ever know." We may, however, insist that the trend of subjective writing since Shakespeare's time would give us greater authority for identifying Hamlet as Shakespeare than Mr. Eliot here seems to acknowledge. For it is precisely when a Symbol is created as a parallel to life rather than as a recipe for obtaining certain effects, that such "Hamletic" confusions generally arise.

through science we face the death of poetry through science. The difficulty lay in the assumption that illusions were inherently "poetic"—whereas they had been made "poetic" by the fact that poets had constructed poetry upon them.[5]

Ambitious writers have selected the "death of tragedy" as an instance of science's destructive effect upon the highest poetry. Tragedy, they have observed, was developed out of a sense of theological or metaphysical stability; man was dignified; he had some direct or personal relationship with the forces of the cosmos; his problems were of vast importance in the universal scheme. But the "illusions" of tragedy are slain by the scientific point of view, which leaves us too humiliated for the noble, godlike posturings of tragedy, wherein man shares the "mystic participation" which M. Lévy-Bruhl attributes to the savage: that sense of the universe as being personally with him or against him. Tragedy is ruined, they say, when the "illusion" of man's personal connection with superhuman processes is lost, when he is looked upon as a mere species of animal that happens to inhabit a planet for a certain number of years between its birth and its extinction. This "death of tragedy" (and thus, the death of the very essence of poetry) is manifested already as an inability to write great tragedies—and in time it will even be manifested as an inability to appreciate the great tragedies already written. Such is, in essence, the position of those who hold to a fundamental opposition between poetry and science—and it has been stated with much fervor and fluency by Mr. Krutch in his volume *The Modern Temper.*

[5] It is not necessary to assume that there is anything inherently dignified about the earth's being the center of the universe. But poets must erect a structure of human dignity upon something, and if the earth happens to be thought the center of the universe, they may find this a convenient belief upon which the structure of human dignity can be erected. Whereupon, in questioning the belief, science may seem to question human dignity itself.

COUNTER-STATEMENT

Mr. Krutch combines under his concept of tragedy both the tragic drama and the tragic spirit. Once a distinction is made between them, however, the issue may look less discouraging. The death of the tragic drama we should attribute to the crumbling of an ideology, as previously explained. The highly fluctuant nature of our thinking at the present time makes more naturally for the essayistic than the dramatic—and the death of tragedy is a natural corollary of this general situation. The question of "poetic illusions" need not enter.

In the matter of the tragic spirit, however, there seems to be no essential abatement at all. For if tragedy is a sense of man's intimate participation in processes beyond himself, we find that science has replaced the older metaphysical structure with an historical structure which gives the individual man ample grounds to feel such participation. What science has taken from us as a personal relationship to the will of Providence, it has re-given as a personal relationship to the slow, unwieldy movements of human society. It is to the greatest credit of Nietzsche that he made this readjustment so thoroughly, turning from the "tragic dignity" of theology to the "tragic dignity" of history, and showing that if there was something "poetic" in the sense of a stable metaphysical structure personally concerned with the fate of man, there can be something equally "poetic" constructed out of the "illusion" or belief now current, the sense of the individual's place in an historical process. In another way the same readjustment was made by Pater in his *Marius the Epicurean,* where the "tragic fallacy" arises from our sense of Marius' close personal relationship to deep alterations in the mentality of peoples. Mr. Krutch himself, had he admitted a distinction between the tragic drama and the tragic spirit, would not have become involved as he does in the task of disproving his own thesis at the close of his book. For having said that tragedy is dead, and that it is dead because the new scientific "truths" have destroyed the tragic "illusions," he ends: "Some small part of the tragic fallacy may be said indeed to be still valid for us, for if we cannot feel ourselves as great as Shakespeare did, if we no longer believe in either our infinite capacities or our importance in the universe, we know at least that we have discovered the trick which has been played upon us and that whatever else we may be we are no longer dupes." He will accept the full responsibilities of this "truth," though the "truth" deprive him of something so edifying, so necessary to the most wholesome human expansiveness, as tragedy: "If death for us and our kind is the inevitable result of our stubbornness, then we can only say, 'So be it.' Ours is a lost cause and there is no place for us in the natural universe, but we are not, for all that, sorry to be human. We should rather die as men than live as animals." He pictures those of his kind watching simpler men who, through having gone less far in their thinking, enjoy certain vital advantages (high among which is "tragic importance"). But though recognizing the advantages that lie with the simple, those of his kind will follow their thoughts even to disaster. Such are Mr. Krutch's obdurate conclusions.

Now, tragedy as a mechanism is based upon a calamitous persistence in one's ways. It is "nobler" when the persistence is due to a moral stability on the part of the hero than when it is due to a mere misunderstanding. What, then, if not the formula for tragedy is this position of Mr. Krutch? He will take a personal stand in relation to an *historic* process (the historic process being in this instance the loss of certain magical and theological or metaphysical "illusions" based upon "non-scientific" systems of causality)—and in this stand he will persist at all hazards. It is good to have a writer display so well the basic machinery for a modern tragedy in a book heralding the death of all tragedy.

COUNTER-STATEMENT

Wordsworth, in his Preface to the *Lyrical Ballads,* has stated the opposite position quite succinctly. If science, he says, "should ever create any material revolution, either direct or indirect, in our condition, and in the impressions which we habitually receive," the poet will carry "sensation into the midst of the objects of the science itself. The remotest discoveries of the Chemist, the Botanist, or Mineralogist, will be as proper objects of the Poet's art as any upon which it can be employed, *if the time should ever come* [our italics] *when these things shall be familiar to us, and the relations under which they are contemplated by the followers of these respective sciences shall be manifestly and palpably material to us as enjoying and suffering beings."* Which is to say, by our present terms, that if an ideology of science obtains general credence, the poet will poetize it by using it for the production of emotional ("human," "poetic") effects. It is not surprising that this statement should have been made by one whose poetry is a simplification, a utilization of "what is left," rather than an attempt to incorporate much new material. For this simplification itself indicated an appreciation of the fact that an ideology was in a state of remaking—it showed a determination to use only so much of the "certain" as remained fairly intact (which was, for him, sensation, or nature, and the sentiment arising from the exaltation of natural processes).

The primary objection to science so far has been the instability of its beliefs, though this does not apply to the general principles of scientific method (the acceptance of skepticism as a major principle of guidance)—and some few doctrines do seem on the road towards "canonization." High among them will probably be the concept of time as a "fourth dimension" (Mr. J. H. Woodger, in his *Biological Principles,* has shown that this concept can serve far beyond the sphere of mathematics). Psychology has perhaps added the word "compensation" as a permanent warning in our terminology of human conduct, and the various aspects of "transference" will probably continue to be stressed. Into the great wilderness of argument and prognostication by statistics we are doubtless permanently launched. A tendency to think in terms of processes will most likely supplant the tendency to think in terms of entities, whereupon "good" and "evil," with all their present concealed shades in our ratings of a "man of character," may be supplanted by such concepts as "adjustment" and "maladjustment." Above all else, the qualities that go with "heroism" will be altered—and not vacillation, but assurance, may be looked upon as the first sign of mental decay. Possibly the Einstein cosmogony will be "naturalized"—whereupon we could have the foundations for a new Dante or Lucretius. And as for dignity, whatever kind of dignity survives will not be based upon a theory of cosmic favoritism, but upon a scheme of human potentialities, a conception of what man "could be" (such a turn from metaphysical to psychological foundations as we have saluted in Nietzsche).

Already there are many new elements to be "poetized." But in so far as the poet "looks before and after," or "binds together by passion and knowledge the vast empire of human society," he cannot at this time be concerned with the new alone. He will, if he is sensitive to the entire situation, retreat slowly (or advance slowly, as one prefers), relinquishing only what must be relinquished, retaining the vocabulary of past beauty so long as he can bring himself to feel its validity, yet never closing his eyes in the interests of comfort and respite, but continually testing the valves and wheels of his poetic mechanism, and not for a moment attempting to conceal from himself the fact that some part or other is outworn. It is quite likely that for each belief science takes from us, some other belief will be placed in its stead. That a new belief seems more "difficult" or less "poetic" need trouble us little, for the difficulty is not inherent, but arises from the fact that we must alter old methods—and if an old belief existed long enough for genial poets to make it poetic, a new and contrary belief must necessarily seem unpoetic until it in turn has been exploited by a poet.

Conventional Form ("categorical expectation"). The matter of conventional form has brought out the extremes of æsthetic acuity and æsthetic bluntness. The rise of conventions may be due to exceptional imaginativeness and accuracy; their preservation may be due to the most inaccurate and unimaginative kinds of pedantry. A reader may, for instance, have come to expect a certain formal contrivance regardless of the effect which this contrivance is best able to produce—and his expectancy may be so imperious that he will condemn the slighting of this form even in an author who is aiming at different effects. Yet in violating a convention, an author is undeniably violating a major tenet of form. For he is disappointing the expectations of his audience; and form, by our definition, resides in the fulfilment of an audience's expectations. The only justification which an author may have for thus breaking faith with his audience is the fact that categorical expectations are very unstable and that the artist can, if his use of the repetitive and progressive principles is authoritative enough, succeed in bringing his audience to a sufficient acceptance of his methods. And as the history of art fully testifies, if the changes in conventional form are introduced to obtain a new stressing, to produce a kind of effect which the violated convention was not well able to produce, but which happens to be more apropos to the contemporary scene, the changes may very rapidly become "canonized" in popular acceptance and the earlier convention may seem the violator of categorical expectancy. All of which may be, in our terminology, the equivalent for Wordsworth's statement that the poet creates the taste by which he is judged.

The issue is further complicated by the fact that resistance to a change in convention may be due to a sensitive appreciation of the convention, to a thorough training in it and familiarity with it. A sonnet in four-foot meter would not scandalize the average salesman. Haydn greatly resented Beethoven's liberties with the sonata-form; yet a modern audience, in finding them acceptable, does not show greater musicianship. The modern audience may simply be insensitive to the issue as Haydn's thorough training enabled him to feel it. For such reasons an innovator may find a more enthusiastic reception among those whose training is defective, particularly if he is aiming at effects which are more apropos to their experiences.

As a handy illustration of the best and weakest aspects of conventional form, we may take the history of the chorus as developed in Greek tragedy. During the incunabula of tragedy, when a tragedy was still the "goat-song," there was not as yet an appreciable element of drama in this predominantly religious festival. The ceremony was wholly choric: there were no individual actors, though the leader of the chorus sometimes contributed antiphonally to the songs. Gradually this antiphonal aspect of the leader was stressed until he split from the chorus entirely, becoming a more or less independent "actor," while a new choric leader took over his former function. Greek tragedy broke clear of these origins and manifested purposes distinct from them when Æschylus, adding a second actor, subordinated the chorus to the dialogue of the two. The result was the tragedy as codified by Aristotle.

The process continued, Sophocles adding a third character to the *dramatis personæ*. In both Æschylus and Sophocles

the chorus was integral to the effects desired. They produced
the sort of drama for which the convention was best fitted.
The ethic meditations of the chorus, the air of solemn comment and understanding they frequently impart to the action, the gravity of their criticism and prophesyings—all
such contribute to the impression of sublimity and determination characteristic of the tragedies at their best. Subsequently, however, the purposiveness of the chorus diminished.
Euripides began to seek effects which the chorus was not
best qualified to produce (effects distinctive of a more "intimate" or realistic drama). At the same time, his art was a
"reversion." He sought to reaffirm some qualities which were
more characteristic of the "goat-song." As is often the case
with the godless, he took a keen interest in the primitive
forms of religion—and thus, at the very time when he was
aiming at effects to which the chorus was not wholly adapted, he restored to the chorus much of the importance which
it had possessed before Æschylus. He stressed the chorus as a
convention, "formalizing" it and divorcing it from the action
of the play. But if Euripides stressed the conventionality of
this convention, in other writers the purely conventional aspects of its appeal are present without such methodological
stressing. At certain periods in their plays, the audience could
expect a choric punctuation of moral maxims, much as the
steps in the plot of a Chinese drama are marked by the striking of gongs. The conventional form was now so slightly
associated with the purposes of drama that, as Aristotle com-
plains, the choric numbers were hardly more than incidental
music: playwrights worked up a store of choric numbers
which they released at fitting intervals, the themes being as
well suited to one place in the play as another, or to one play
as another.

When the continuity of the tragedy was restored in England, the chorus was at first preserved (owing, it is said, to the

maintaining of this convention in the plays of Seneca, who was the model for English playwrights). In time the chorus was dropped entirely: the Elizabethan playwrights were nearer to the effects of Euripides than of Æschylus—and with the tragedy now so far from its origins, and with an audience which had no training in the ways of classic tragedy, the chorus lacked any authority for inclusion on the grounds of conventional form. As Elizabethan tragedies were not written to be sung through masks, so they were not written in a vein in which the unreality of a chorus' moralizings could have been anything but an obstacle. (Perhaps Wagner's "music-drama" is, in this one respect, closer to the æsthetic of the Greek tragedy.)

Elizabethan tragedy did, however, seek ceremonious effects which were akin to those of the chorus. The proscenium speech was not merely "tolerated": it was requisite to such effects. Diction, in all the distinctly tragic scenes, was cast in a mold to suggest the grandiose, the heightened. Tragedy was no longer sung—but it was ranted. Hence appropriate conventions were developed—the set speech, or monologue, being one of them. There is good cause to believe that the monologue was enjoyed exactly as an aria in Italian opera. Subsequently, as tragedy developed towards the "realistic," becoming the tragedy not of exceptional people but of "you and me," the appeal of the frankly recitative monologue diminished. After being *enjoyed* as conventional form, it was next *tolerated* as conventional form, and finally developed into a mere convenience for slovenly playwrights, a kind of "aside" for imparting necessary information to the audience, whereas the new effects required the complete elimination of such a device. It clung, however, until the time of Ibsen— and fittingly, was not dismissed here until Ibsen turned from verse to prose.

Yet as evidence that the conventional forms, at the heyday

of their usage, serve a very accurate purpose, we have An-dreyev's restoration of the chorus' function in *The Life of Man*. In this play Andreyev sought, though imperfectly, to regain the effects of Æschylean and Sophoclean tragedy—the sense of fatalistic guidance which each of these play-wrights utilized so well to make the audience feel that not the author, but the nature of things, was moving the story. Thus, Andreyev invented the character of Someone in Gray Called He, who stood about the edges of the play, aloof from its action, prophesying, moralistically commenting upon the allegorical destiny of these humble characters, and in all important respects except the matter of eloquence rediscover-ing the purpose of the Greek chorus as an instrument in procuring one kind of dramatic effect. And similarly, we might make clearer the functional value of the monologue in Shakespeare by pointing out that his tragic effects ap-proach those of Greek tragedy in so far as a character's medi-tations upon his own fate can substitute for the part of the detached chorus in Æschylus and Sophocles (though witches, ghosts, and portents are also greatly relied upon to make the audience feel more the hand of the cosmos than that of the playwright).

In summary we may note the dual aspect of conventional form: It thrives when the audience expects it and also re-quires the kind of effects which it is best able to produce; but it becomes an obstacle if it remains as categorical expect-ancy at a time when different effects are aimed at. But we should note two further aspects of the subject:

First: the absence of marked conventional contrivances often leads to a kind of "one-time" convention which is liked purely as an innovation. Thus, we may see one play con-structed as an *"aria da capo,"* another borrowing quick change of scene from the motion picture, another built upon the convention that people speak out their innermost thoughts (restoration of the aside); or for a season we restore the old "thriller" of the 'eighties; or a great musician will adopt some historical manner for fifteen minutes—and in all such cases we enjoy the convention purely because of its transiency. If another man repeated the performance, we should thunder against him as eagerly as we applauded the first. Yet a convention is most fruitful, obviously, when it is stable enough for many men to converge upon the exploitation of it.[6] (It is for this reason that the stock characters of Broadway drama are to be taken seriously; for how can they, by the sheer laws of probability, be used so often without something good eventually coming of them?)

Our second consideration is: Categorical expectancy does not only make for inclusions; it also makes for exclusions. In expecting how things *will be,* we expect by implication how they *will not be.* Much of the difficulty with imaginative prose today lies in the fact that our categorical expectations require a manner poorly adapted to the fuller potentialities of prose. We are at the end of a "conversational" trend in prose, a trend which has proved its high value in purely informative writing, but acts as an impoverishment when the informative is not primarily aimed at. Nothing more clearly displays the occasional tyranny and arbitrariness of conventional form than this contemporary insistence upon a "narrative" style of prose. If a prose-writer departs from it, he is called artificial, though not one of his sentences has the obvious artificiality of verse (this verse, meanwhile, being

[6] The matter of the Greek chorus may give us some insight as to the nature of "invention" in art. The Greek chorus was not "invented" by Æschylus; it was adapted to a new purpose. In all probability, had the whole idea of the chorus been an innovation, he could not have succeeded in making his use of the chorus generally acceptable. Similarly, in adding a second actor, he did not innovate, but simply carried a process one step further. An artist probably works nearest to impunity if his innovations are adaptations of this sort.

deemed "natural"). The reader of modern prose is ever on guard against "rhetoric," yet the word, by lexicographer's definition, refers but to "the use of language in such a way as to produce a desired impression upon the hearer or reader."

Rhetoric. As a final instance of the hazards of convention, we might with profit examine the history of this word's decay. In accordance with the definition we have cited, effective literature could be nothing else but rhetoric: thus the resistance to rhetoric *qua* rhetoric must be due to a faulty diagnosis. To an extent, this resistance is a revolt against an over-emphasizing of the traditionally ceremonious (since inferior "rhetoricians," in their attempt to be "eloquent," confined themselves to such material as had been made "eloquent" by earlier and more talented artists). As such the resistance is wholesome and commendable enough. But much of the resistance is also due to a mistake in critical nomenclature. As artists no longer wished to produce the kinds of effect which the devices of the rhetoricians were designed to produce, they overshot the mark—and to turn against a specific method of specific rhetoricians, they persuaded themselves that they were turning against rhetoric *in toto*. Thus, since the rhetorical procedure had become identified as the art of appeal, the artist who chose to appeal in other ways felt that he had given up any attempt to appeal at all. This led, above all, to a denigration of form (formal devices being a major portion of the rhetorician's lore); and the one factor in keeping such denigration of form from doing great damage was the artist's tendency to preserve many more aspects of form than he was aware of. Once again the issue was improperly diagnosed—and in revolting against certain kinds of form, the artist persuaded himself that he was revolting against form in general.

Now, slogans are always bungling. They must somewhat

overstate their case to get what they are after. And the over-statement of the case against "rhetoric" undeniably served a salutary end. But it has left us with too wide a distrust, and a tendency to discountenance the use of pronounced formal contrivances even in a writer who might use them to produce such effects as they were designed to produce. If the respect clung too long, the distrust now threatens equally to outlast its usefulness. In particular this distrust militates against the retention or rediscovery of old values which cannot be permanently eliminated without considerable impoverishment of art. Their temporary elimination was wholesome, since it made other emphases possible, enabling us to develop an "imperceptible" variety of prose which flowers in the information-giving of the best journalism and narratives. But in this matter the zest of discovery has long since abated; the billions of "controversial" words turned out yearly by our country's presses cannot, as sentences, delight us further. The major tenet of eloquence (maximum of formal and Symbolic "charge") must be reaffirmed if prose *qua* prose is to be enjoyed. Yet such a reaffirmation must overcome the resistance of "categorical expectancy," must temporarily at least violate the principles of conventional form, must risk seeming "unnatural" until the present decrees as to the "natural" are undone.

The reversal is not unthinkable. Already an objection to the barrenness of much modern prose is arising in many quarters. And though a critic recently asked himself "by what confusion the contemporaries of Mozart were led to praise as 'natural' musical compositions as elaborately formal as his," it almost seems that in the few months since this sentence was written, Mozart's musical compositions have again become "natural."

So, to capitulate: One aims at effects; whatever effects he desires, he can in all humility be assured that they are "natural," since his desire could not possibly be anything other than natural; and if he finds the present categorical expectancies obstructive to his purposes, he may be justified in violating these expectancies and in allowing his procedures to be viewed as an oddity, as peripheral, on the chance that other men may eventually join him and by their convergence make such procedures the "norm."

CURRICULUM CRITICUM

SINCE one can sometimes make a position clearer by showing its place in a "curve" of development, there is the possibility that this first book, on being reissued, might be placed in terms of later books written by the same author. Also, when one has been through changes in the mental climate, a graph of his responses to the veerings of history might be at least clinically of value. (Let the slogan be: Challenge none, apologize to none, explain to any who will listen.)

Counter-Statement shows signs of its emergence out of adolescent fears and posturings, into problems of early manhood (problems morbidly intensified by the market crash of '29). The rôle, or *persona* of the author seems not that of father, or even of brother, but of conscientiously wayward son (whom the Great Depression compelled to laugh on the other side of his face).

He had early decided that, ideally, for each of Shakespeare's dramatic tactics, modern thought should try to find the corresponding critical formulation. But he soon came to see that any such orderly unfolding of the past into the present would be greatly complicated, if not made irrelevant and even impossible, by the urgencies and abruptnesses of social upheaval.

After *Counter-Statement* came "Auscultation, Creation, and Revision," a short book or long essay still in manuscript. Half-analytically, half-dithyrambically, it sought to resist the mounting sociological emphasis in criticism, even while dealing with problems of "orientation" to which the author had been made uncomfortably sensitive by the brusque contrast between the beginning of Hoover's presidency and its end. As point of departure the work quarreled with the shift in Edmund Wilson's *Axel's Castle*—and it sought to reassert a kind of æsthetic mysticism that came to a head in a "manifesto-like" appreciation of Li Tai Po's lyric, "Drinking Alone in the Moonlight." (It clung to the thought that lunar poet and poetic moon are synthesized in the image of the poet's moon-cast shadow.) The title referred to three stages of production: (1) the heart-conscious kind of listening, or vigilance, that precedes expression; (2) the expression in its unguarded simplicity; (3) modification of the expression, in the light of more complicated after-thoughts.

As a companion-piece to this, there was a shorter essay built around a conceit: It concerned a writer who, in early spring during one of the intensely Depression-ridden years, was leaving the city with his family for a retreat in the country. The city was somehow in upheaval, and the train pulled out of the station just as the first of a pursuing mob hove into sight. The writer, sitting by a window on the south side of the coach, emerged from shadow into steady sunlight as the train got under way.

The essay also included a vision of the dispossessed, gathering in petition by a rich man's door. The one editor to whom this essay was submitted rejected it on the grounds that it was "unreal," as indeed it was. It ended on a quotation from a self-pronouncing Bible, with diacritical marks on all the "hard" words.

However, this quotation was acrimoniously pitted against a contemporary stockmarket operator's reference to Damascus in connection with some oil deals. And in his next phase, the critic took avid notes on corporate devices whereby business enterprisers had contrived to build up empires by purely financial manipulations. (These manipulations were sometimes useful, sometimes irrelevant, sometimes positively harmful, to the real services performed by the operating companies above which such purely symbolic superstructures were erected.) When the course of his studies led the author to the records of the Pujo Investigation undertaken by a Congressional committee, he saw that the answers to his questions had been amply supplied years before he had even thought to ask them—so he moved on.

He now widened his speculations to include a concern with problems of motivation in general. (Writings by Jeremy Bentham, in particular, had indicated to him ways whereby linguistic and sociological inquiries could be merged.) The first completed manuscript of this material he called "Treatise on Communication." In its final, published form, it was called *Permanence and Change: An Anatomy of Purpose,* the publisher having objected to the earlier title on the grounds that it made the work sound like a textbook on telegraphy. Communication, interpretation, orientation, integration, coöperation, transformation, simplification—such are its concerns. The author now stressed interdependent, social, or collective aspects of meaning, in contrast with the individualistic emphasis of his earlier Æstheticist period. (The earlier individualism had itself been modified by association in

CURRICULUM CRITICUM

a pranksome kind of literary "gang morality" loosely linking several young writers who liked to think of themselves as a monster-loving "advance guard.")

Unfortunately for the standing of this book in these uneasy times, the family of key words that includes "communication," "communicant," "community," and "communion" also has a well-known relative now locally in great disgrace—and the experimental author, then contritely eager to think of himself as part of an over-all partnership, had plumped grandly for that word, too. Accordingly, statements that concern humanistic integration and cultural reconstruction in general were sometimes localized in terms of this one problematical "-ism." And we hardly need add that, though the term is traditionally liberal and idealistic, with usages extending across whole millennia of history, it has recently been endowed with egregiously particular associations, by both the adherents and the enemies of one specific faction in contemporary world politics.

The term had particularly suited the author's poetico-political speculations of that time since he was much concerned with the thought that secular communities might be formed after the analogy of monastic orders, or of the many theocratic or theologically tinged colonies that were attempted during the earlier stages of our nation's history, all of them variously modifying private property in the direction of possessions that were jointly owned or jointly served. (One such that had been left purely in the stage of Utopian planning was the "aspheterist" project which the idealist poets, Coleridge and Southey, had talked of founding on the banks of the Susquehanna, in a naïve hope that the rules of communal ownership might "make virtue inevitable.")

Incidentally, looking back over the work, in the light of his later concern with "rebirth-rituals," the author finds that a purely imaginal process underlies the conceptualizing. The book is in three parts, the middle part being transitional (and thereby appropriately dealing with such kinds of fragmentation and double-vision as go with a shift from one integration to another). The work starts with talk of a fish in water; the transitional section is a kind of emergence; but the final coming-clear, in a rationale of "resimplification," leads to a corresponding uneasiness, as regards the very perspectivalism which the book had advocated—and in the last sentence we are admonished that "men build their cultures by huddling together, nervously loquacious, at the edge of an abyss." In the weeks (and even months) following the completion of the book, the author had a painfully obsessive sense of distance, as though everything he saw, or everyone he spoke to, were behind glass.

Permanence and Change was written in 1932-33. It was published in 1935. *Attitudes Toward History* followed (published in 1937). Thinking of kind rather than degree, we might say that *P&C* is to *ATH* as Plato's *Republic* is to his *Laws*. That is, just as the *Republic* deals with an ideal State, and the *Laws* deals with a real one, so *P&C* thinks of communication in terms of ideal coöperation, whereas *ATH* would characterize tactics and patterns of conflict typical of actual human associations. The middle or transitional section of *P&C* had been built about a somewhat Nietzschean concept, "perspective by incongruity," a kind of vision got by seeing one order in terms of another. *ATH* hinges about a particular perspective by incongruity, the "bureaucratization of the imaginative" (a formula for the imperfections that arise in human societies when ideal ends are translated into material means). The more realistic emphasis reflects the fact that the author had begun to get a closer view of the ways in which projects for social amelioration work out practically—and he opted for a somewhat perverse kind of Neo-Stoicism, a "comic" resignation to the inevitability of "progress" with its attendant scrambles. The principles of "acceptance" and "rejection" here featured led eventually into a study of the negative command as the moral center of man's linguistic genius. The book summed up its sociology in a "Dictionary of Pivotal Terms" that aims to isolate major moments in the dialectics of allegiance and faction.

We might sum up the change from *P&C* to *ATH* thus: *ATH* reflects the author's growing awareness that private property is to be studied as a function rather than as a thing, and that it prevails functionally whenever specific rights or rewards are assigned to one person rather than to others in accordance with that person's meeting of certain obligations as defined by the laws and customs of the given social order. In this sense, all reasonable individual expectancies, on the basis of service rendered, are "private properties." Accordingly, manifestations as varied as jobs, honors, and familial affection could all be rated as kinds of private property, with corresponding kinds of personal gratification, that in turn had their corresponding kinds of personal unrest insofar as the gratifications were, or seemed to be, threatened or withheld. But though the author is asking the reader not to linger at any one stage as we thus hurry through several stages,

CURRICULUM CRITICUM

all of which should (in a final "telescoping") be treated as modifica-
tions of one another, he would pause long enough to remind that he
is by no means "disclaiming" the *P&C*-steps that led him into his
ATH-ism (and thus subsequently into more complicated beliefs and
sufferances). For a given problem of location, one calculus is handier
than another; and the author would still fondly contend that, as
regards matters of communication in general, *P&C* meets requirements that *ATH* cannot meet. (For instance, the analysis of metaphor,
or "analogy"; the formulating of a notable stylistic principle embodied
in the works of Nietzsche, and the applying of this to the analysis of
"perspective" and "rebirth"; analysis of the part played by "piety"
and "impiety" in matters of "orientation.")

The next book, *Philosophy of Literary Form: Studies in Symbolic
Action* (1941) is mainly a collection of essays and reviews published
at various times over the previous decade. But the long titular piece
aims both to give a summarization of the author's notions about the
symbolic function of literary forms and to sketch a technique for the
analysis of a work in its nature as a structure of organically inter-
related terms. Whereas the stress in *Counter-Statement* had been
rhetorical (form as the arousing and fulfilling of an audience's expectations), the stress now was upon the work in its internality (the
"equations" which it inevitably embodies in its action as an evolving
unity). The method was somewhat phenomenological in aim, seeking
to get at the psychological depth of a work through the sheer comparison of its surfaces. The method was illustrated by reference to
various works, the analysis of Hitler's *Mein Kampf* being perhaps the
fullest instance; and there was a basic concern with Freud and
Coleridge. The last item in the book, "Dialectician's Hymn," defines
Dialectic in somewhat piously Neo-Platonist accents, though the
author knows of no reader who ever got so far into his text.

Meanwhile, the early notes on corporate devices had gradually
been resumed, but in a much more general form. They now concerned all sorts of tactics whereby people sought to outwit themselves
and one another in social intercourse (tactics ranging from world-
shaking diplomatic maneuvers down to the minutiæ of drawing-room
repartee, social "cat-fights," bland insults, and the like). The notion
was that this "post-Machiavellian" lore should be treated in a book
"On Human Relations" designed to round out the concerns of *P&C*
and *ATH*. However, when the author sought to write up his notes,
more preparatory ground-work was found necessary; and *A Grammar*

of Motives (1945) resulted. *A Rhetoric of Motives* followed in 1950. *A Symbolic of Motives* is now in progress. These three *Motivorum* books deal with linguistic structures in their *logical, rhetorical,* and *poetic* dimensions respectively. And they will require a fourth volume, probably specifically entitled "On Human Relations," stressing the *ethical* dimension of language. (As things thus turned out, the devices that were to be the beginning of the project are postponed until its end.)

Gradually, engagements in lecturing and teaching had given a more pedagogical turn to the author's interests in criticism. In particular, he had had the advantage of friendly controversy with the "Neo-Aristotelians" during a term at the University of Chicago; and his happy and helpful connection with Bennington College began in 1943. So, though he has written no textbooks in the formal sense, he became more and more concerned with specifically educational problems. For instance, the long section on "The Philosophic Schools" was not in the original version of his *Grammar,* but was added after experiences in tutoring certain students who wanted to study philosophy.

The *Grammar* is the grounding of the *Motivorum* project. It devolves about five key "Dramatist" terms (that were discovered late in the investigation, though it seems so obvious that the author should have begun with them, as he does begin, in the revised, published version of the original manuscript). Here a poor mathematician seeks in his way to attain the generalizing ways of pure mathematics. That is, he asks: What must we be prepared to look for, when anyone is saying why anybody did anything? (His manuscript was originally entitled "On the Imputing of Motives.")

The *Rhetoric* returns to the problems of bureaucracy, but now considers them in terms of "hierarchy" and its "mysteries," antitheses of association and dissociation thus being modified by a concern with the "pyramidal" nature of social orders, as these affect consciousness and expression. (It concerns the relations that characterize a ladder of Mr. Bigs and Mr. Littles, all along the line, up and down, with the "magic" of these.) The *Symbolic* will seek to treat of further problems that have to do with the intrinsic analysis of texts. The whole project aims to round out an analysis of language in keeping with the author's favorite notion that, man being the specifically language-using animal, an approach to human motivations should be made through the analysis of language. It seeks for observations that, while central to the study of any given expression in its internality, also have reference

CURRICULUM CRITICUM

to human quandaries and human foibles generally. The project begins in and never far departs from (since it never wants far to depart from) the Aristotelian notion of poetry as *cathartic*.

The author believes that, for all the occasional immaturity of some attitudes in his *Counter-Statement*, the book adequately supplies an introduction into his later concerns. (In one sense it has an advantage over them, particularly for readers who prefer leaps from *A* to *E*, as against the more laborious business of going back and seeking to supply intermediate steps *B*, *C*, and *D*.)

We might also mention, in the interests of thoroughness, two works of fiction (*The White Oxen* and *Towards a Better Life*) which the author published early in his career and which, whatever one may think of their intrinsic merit, have been of great value to him, because he can now remember them as from without, whereas once he experienced them drastically from within—and he has found this double vision useful for his analysis of motives. The same goes for verses that he has written now and then over the years. He hopes to publish a short selection of this material soon.

In sum: The books take their start from a principle of form typified in drama. This principle was capable of development with regard to intrinsic analysis of texts; also it led into the study of verbal expression with regard to the non-verbal situations in which such expression takes place. Since "symbolic action" really is a kind of action empirically observable, the author contends that a terminology thus developed in conformity with the forms of drama is not the sheer use of analogy, the extended ramifying of a metaphor, but is strictly literal in reference. Man *is* the specifically symbol-using animal, and a "Dramatistic" theory of motives is systematically grounded in this view of human essence. While such analysis of language and of human motives at some points overlaps upon literary criticism in the strict sense of the term, at many other points it leads into inquiries not central to literary criticism—and sometimes literary critics have quarreled with the author for neglecting the problems of literary criticism proper, whereas no other course was open to him, insofar as he wanted also to discuss symbolic motivations and linguistic action in general.

K. B.

Los Altos, California
January, 1953

COUNTER-STATEMENT

Since this article was written (in 1953), a collection of verse was published (*Book of Moments: Poems 1915–1954*). As the Foreword has it: "Lyrics are 'moments' insofar as they pause to sum up a motive. They are designed to express and evoke a unified attitude towards some situation more or less explicitly implied." And self-protectively the author quotes from Emerson: "Our moods do not believe in each other."

The next book of criticism, *The Rhetoric of Religion: Studies in Logology* (1961), is a methodic attempt to disclose how "words about God" (theology) can be applied to a wholly empirical end, for the light they throw upon "words about words" ("logology"). "The subject of religion falls under the head of *rhetoric* in the sense that rhetoric is an art of *persuasion,* and religious cosmogonies are designed, in the last analysis, as exceptionally thoroughgoing modes of persuasion." The book is in four parts. The first treats of six fundamental analogies between "words" and "The Word." The second analyzes "Verbal Action in St. Augustine's *Confessions"* (a particularly relevant text since Augustine began as an expert in pagan rhetoric and later adapted his skills to ecclesiastical purposes). The third, focussing upon the first three chapters of Genesis, asks how the story of the Creation and the Fall (Order and its liabilities) translates logical relationships into terms of temporal sequence. And the fourth part, "Prologue in Heaven," is an imaginary dialogue in which The Lord explains to Satan what we must expect, once the word-using animal has been created. Satan is pictured as a young hothead who is a great admirer of The Lord (when he learns that the earth-people will put The Lord's name on their money, he exclaims "How revolting!"). For the dialogue "took place" before anything had gone wrong among the angelic hordes. The author feels justifiably proud that, in these sorry days, he at least contributed towards an improved version of hell.

In 1964 came two volumes edited by Stanley Edgar Hyman: *Terms for Order*, and *Perspectives by Incongruity*. These are selections from items already published, though some pieces were out of print. The emphasis is mainly on the literary aspects of my work; fiction and verse are also included. In particular we might mention "Fact, Inference, and Proof in the Analysis of Literary Symbolism." This essay gives rules of thumb for the "indexing" of a work, using for this purpose James Joyce's *Portrait of the Artist as a Young Man*.

In 1966 came the republication of the early novel, *Towards a Better Life*. Its subtitle, "Being a Series of Declamations, or Epistles," might indicate why, in current cant, the book could be called somewhat of an "anti-novel." It was so designed that a plot might gradually emerge from a context of "lamentation, rejoicing, beseechment, admonition, sayings, and invective." Since the manner is grotesque (in its incongruous juxtaposing of the solemn and the comic), I feel inclined to go along with Denis Donoghue's judgment (in *Encounter*, October 1967) that it is to be classed among those works in which man is "dangling, dissociated, an alien." And Mr. Donoghue seems somewhat inclined to go along with my notion that it is in the bin I'd call "sprout-out-of-rot literature." Enigmatically, it contains in germ many implications that the author has subsequently translated into explicit critical theorizing on motives, both poetic and general.

In the same year there also appeared the collection: *Language as Symbolic Action: Essays on Life, Literature, and Method*. The entries are all in keeping with my notion that, as regards readers who might love criticism for its own sake, the alignment is not just life-and-literature, but life-literature-

and-method. It comprises several specific analyses of literary texts (dramas, novels, poems), and articles on the relation that concepts of poetic action in particular bear to the quandaries of the human situation in general. A methodic concern with the resources and embarrassments of terms heads up in a "logological" or "dramatistic" involvement with such unwieldy matters as: myth, poetry, philosophy, mind, body, the unconscious, catharsis, and transcendence. Various attempts are made at analyzing a work by "prophesying after·the event," an expository procedure intended to reveal the logic of a symbolic act by proposing postulates in accordance with which it can be "generated."

The publication of this book has once again modified the *Motivorum* project as a whole. I had first planned a trilogy: (1) universal relationships, as in my *Grammar of Motives;* (2) partisan relationships, and their modes of real or apparent transcending, as in my *Rhetoric of Motives;* and (3) a *Symbolic of Motives,* the study of individual identity. This third volume would include both poetic and ethical dimensions, inasmuch as both the character of the individual poem and the character of the individual person embody "equations" (explicit or implicit assumptions as to what fits with what). At some stages along the way, I saw this third volume splitting into two. But now that so many of my speculations about Poetics have been treated in the theoretical and analytical pieces of which *Language as Symbolic Action* is comprised, I dare believe that I can revert to my original plan and finish the project in one more book.

Collected Poems: 1915–1967 followed. Here, to the reprinting of the earlier "moments" is added a later assortment that, for a while, I thought of calling *The Orphan's Cheek,* a title suggested by a Spanish proverb, "The barber learns on the orphan's cheek." One can be simultaneously the apprentice and the waif on which he learns. But while hesitating, I wrote a poem entitled "Introduction to What"—and that seemed to fill the bill for the lot. Then I pulled out five for a section "In Conclusion," though several others could have served equally well as variations on the same theme. In many of the verses the author thinks of his "morbid Selph" as "lost among the monsters of machinery and politics, and hardly other than an insect which, while making tiny noises after the nature of its kind, could never know when some huge creature of the forest, heavy-footed as a mastodon, might just happen to stamp him out, merely in the course of going on its way." But alas, that's not exactly the mood of *The Iliad,* though wars are still with us.

Next came *The Complete White Oxen,* a reissue of the early stories, with additions, including a much later autobiographical departure, "The Anaesthetic Revelation of Herone Liddell" (first published in *The Kenyon Review* of Autumn 1957). Most of the early stories were written in an orthodoxly realistic mode. But outcroppings of fantasy began to emerge. To a mildly friendly critic these suggested the name of Lord Dunsany. To an unfriendly one they suggested the Adventures of Little Nemo, whose wondrous wanderings were recorded each week (for children actual or grown-up) in the Sunday supplements near the start of our century. I think it can be shown now that the narratives involved a fluctuant mixture of realism, naturalism, formalism, and (as regards tinkering with conventional form) incipient surrealism. Their author believes that the eye reads too fast for several of these pieces, which fare best if read at a pace natural to the speaking voice. Hence their frequent inclusion of verse.

And now the new paperback edition of *Counter-Statement,* as was, except for this addendum. The step from the opening chapter, "Three Adepts of 'Pure' Literature," to the next essay, "Psychology and Form," clearly indicates a turn from the stress upon self-expression to a stress upon communication. And all that follows can be properly treated as the tracking down of the implications inherent in this turn. In later works I have added an explicit concern with the kind of *consummation* that is inherent in this very process of "tracking down the implications of a nomenclature." As for the confirmed distrust of technologism that informs the chapter entitled "Program," with its speculations "as to which emotions and attitudes should be stressed, and which slighted, in the aesthetic adjustment to the particular conditions of today" (that is, 1931): social and scientific developments since then have made obvious many new and altered implications of this same position. High among them are those developments that complicate my thesis by having nearly eliminated whatever kinds of agriculture failed to keep abreast of industrial "progress."

What next? There is still the rounding-out of the *Motivorum* project. It includes a set of "devices," the main body of which I collected during the Thirties and Forties. Though I have used some of this material in classrooms and in academic lectures, the only published portion is an essay, "Rhetoric— Old and New," originally printed in *The Journal of General Education* (April 1951), and recently reprinted in *New Rhetorics,* edited by Martin Steinmann, Jr. Also, corresponding to the essays collected in *Language as Symbolic Action,* there is a set of already published pieces which could be assembled under the title of *The Rhetorical Situation,* though they'd need an introductory or concluding essay methodically concerned with the problems of classification that necessarily plague any such project (since the modes of rhetorical appeal can be stated in highly *generalized* terms, yet any given act of exhortation arises out of a context so immediately urgent as to be *unique*).

And then, if the author lasts, and the bombs hold off, there is the inchoate possibility of an avowal involving literal

CURRICULUM CRITICUM

memories, deliberate fictions, and diaristic accidents encountered during the writing. The author is grateful for a grant from the Rockefeller Foundation, towards this end. Whether or not the plan eventuates, the design is mentioned merely to indicate how, if all went as ideally intended, things would shape up. There's that word *consummation* again!

K.B.

Adams House, Cambridge, Mass., Nov. 1967